The Career Ninja Mindset®

5 Precision Moves To Win At Work

by ALEXIS KING

Published by
Hybrid Global Publishing
333 E 14th Street #3C New York, NY 10003

Manufactured in the United States of America, or the United Kingdom when distributed elsewhere.

King, Alexis
The Career Ninja Mindset®: 5 Steps to Success in Work and Life

ISBN: ###
eBook: ##
LCCN: ###

Cover design by: ##
Copyediting by: ##
Interior design by: Amit Dey
Author photo by: ##

TABLE OF CONTENTS

CHAPTER 1

OUT OF THE BLUE

I spent nearly twenty years in banking. Moving up with each promotion, creating every appearance of a secure career. By the time I was thirty, I had a BMW, vacationed in Aruba regularly, and had completed my MBA, bought a condo, and paid off most of my student debt. I was following the generational expectations of "Get a good education, get a steady job, buy a house, settle down." My success ensured my parents didn't need to worry about my ability to support myself in case I didn't land a good husband, too.

Then I got laid off.

Out of nowhere, the bank where I worked eliminated 650 of us in one day. None of us saw it coming.

If you are sitting there thinking, *Poor Alexis,* don't. I've recovered and am doing better than ever. It wasn't an easy path, though. There were no miracles or unexpected inheritances to give me a financial cushion. It has been a rewarding journey of hard work and self-discovery. More than once I have thought, *If only I'd known* this *sooner. If only someone had told me.*

I've heard it said, "Become the person you needed when you were younger," which is why it is so important for me to be that person for you. In this book, you will read about finding your joy and passion. My joy is sharing what I've learned about navigating career and life transitions.

Getting laid off was the catalyst for discovering that my passion is coaching and training others.

I have taken my life lessons and turned them into a process, which if you adopt, will enable you to navigate your own path with agility.

If you are sitting there thinking, *I'm not going to get laid off. I perform a critical function. I've been here too long. Even if it were possible, I'd see it coming... a mile away.* Think again. Two of my friends, one a partner in her firm and both earning over six figures, were let go by their company last month.

If you think layoffs only happen at manufacturing companies or start-ups, think again. Last year, all the major tech companies underwent major layoffs. This year, many of them have already announced thousands of additional layoffs. Skilled workers in just about every industry are losing their jobs. The explosion in AI adoption is putting writers and creatives out of work at blinding rates. Job security probably ceased with your parents' generation.

The good news

There is something you can do to protect yourself from all of this career uncertainty. Be prepared. It's that simple, but not necessarily that easy. The process described on the following pages will help you make a career change, advance your career, or launch your dream business. The skills you incorporate will help you with more than an unexpected change or setback. They will help you level up, find passion, and lead a more fulfilled life.

If you live in an area that is prone to natural disasters, such as hurricanes and wildfires, or have even just watched the news coverage, you may have heard the term "bugout bag." Originally military slang, *bugout* means to leave a place quickly. Bugout bags include essential items you will need if you have to leave your home suddenly: ID, flashlight, change of clothes, bottled water, energy bars, money, keys, phone, and laptop.

While it may seem overdramatic to compare job loss with a natural disaster, the skills to cope with both of these unexpected events are similar, and I learned them when I had to move on from my layoff. The bottom line for both of these situations is: *You need to be ready.*

Being prepared will serve you no matter what your career or personal life is. If you want a promotion, be prepared. If you want to move to another city, to another coast, or to another country, be prepared. If you want to pursue a passion project, be prepared.

The strategies you find in this book aren't merely coping mechanisms for the unexpected; they will show you how to plan and prepare for all of life's transitions. Think of them as the essential items you want to pack in your career bugout bag. The good news is that by learning these strategies, you may not have to make sudden and stressful moves. You will be able to implement plans that assure smooth and confident transitions. Plus, you'll be ready to seize any unexpected opportunities.

I took two actions that were immediate game changers for me. I began working with a business coach (we'll talk more about that later) and I enrolled in courses to gain new skills.

I chose a course focused on strengthening my real estate skills. In the class, each participant shared their background and what had brought them to this point in their careers. After I detailed a little about my career path, one of the other students commented, "You are like a career transition ninja."

Ninja? What does he mean? When he noticed the puzzled look on my face, he explained he meant I was adaptable, like the traditional Japanese ninjas we read about in history books.

What do you picture when you hear or see the word *ninja*? A warrior sneaking around the grounds at night, dressed in black? Or maybe you remember the Teenage Mutant Ninja Turtles. While the characters bear no resemblance to historical ninjas, their entrance into the vernacular of the '80s and '90s made us all aware of the term. Leonardo, Donatello, Raphael, and Michelangelo stepped off the comic book page to become action figures. Next, they transitioned to their own animated television series, then leaped into video games, and finally, expanded into larger-than-life movie characters. They, too, were certainly adaptable.

After that day in class, I read anything I could find online about real ninjas. And the more I discovered, the more apt I found the "career transition ninja" label to be.

Real ninjas are even more intriguing and inspiring than any stereotype. The Japanese ninja, or more accurately, *Shinobi no Mono*, is someone with stealth and perseverance. The first historical references to ninjas date back to 12th-century Japan. Unlike samurai, trained warriors from noble families, ninjas came from families of tradesmen and farmers. There were also female ninjas called *kunoichi*. Warlords employed ninjas to gather intelligence about their enemies, so they needed to be skillful, nimble, and adaptable. I found I was liking this ninja imagery more and more.

Ninjas and their skills were in such demand that by the 14th century, the first of forty-nine specialized schools opened in Japan. Students trained on how to use meditation to overcome fear. They studied astronomy, medicine, poisons, code breaking, rock climbing, and lock picking. While ninjas were more commonly used for espionage, they also received training in martial arts and how to fashion weapons out of common farm tools. Their training prepared them for any situation.

Disguised as dancers or humble servants, the *kunoichi* had the upper hand when it came to gaining entry into an enemy camp. People often dismissed women as harmless. This gave them an advantage over their male counterparts as spies and assassins. As their reputation spread, *shinobi* and *kunoichi* were so highly regarded, many were able to rise to the heights of society.

While I am not promoting espionage and assassination, the ability to infiltrate and assimilate is certainly important. Think about it: Working your way into a new company is a form of infiltration. And assimilation is absolutely critical in adapting and accommodating a new corporate culture.

I identified with the *kunoichi* because of their eagerness to learn a variety of skills to accomplish their objectives. I asked myself: *Is my ability to adapt and overcome part of my nature? Was I born with it?* To a degree, yes, but you can acquire these are skills. I've put together a list of the strengths and strategies I've used to propel myself through my life and career success. Once I identified my process, I named it *The Career Ninja Mindset*®.

It's time to develop your skills

Now, I'm on a mission to share my method with you so you can learn how to *recognize*, develop, and use your natural ninja skills. No nunchucks necessary. I emphasize the word "recognize" because we often overlook skills and abilities we already possess. Using my preexisting skills, I was able to make a successful transition out of banking into a completely different field, without having to get another degree.

For this book, I've included stories of my own successful transitions and showcased composite stories from people whom I have helped to advance their careers.

These success stories inspired me to write this book so I can share the steps I've developed and used to create a rewarding life I love. Have fun reading it. It is not a textbook; you do not need to master one skill before moving onto the next. Although I wrote the section on the Five P's in a tactical order, you are free to scan the Table of Contents and choose the chapters that appeal to you. However, I recommend you read the complete book, because you will find useful information throughout and see how each skill integrates with another.

I'm excited to hear about your experiences using The Career Ninja Mindset® and have included my contact information at the end of the book so you can share your stories with me, and I can celebrate your wins with you.

I encourage you to always be receptive to learning new things—which includes adding to and strengthening your skill set. I came to understand that this is the secret to how I've progressed and how things turned around for me. In the chapters that follow, I will introduce you to, and train you just like a ninja, using five steps that will speed up your career and help you achieve professional success. My method will prepare you to move confidently through any and all of life's transitions. Are you ready to begin?

CHAPTER 2

WHAT ARE THE FIVE P'S OF SUCCESS?

We plan some of life's transitions—like buying a new home—while others take us by surprise—like getting laid off. While developing The Career Ninja Mindset®, I identified five steps—The Five P's of Success—that will accelerate your career, and which you can use to glide from one life situation to another. The following steps will empower you to pursue your passion, whether you want to try a new creative pursuit, scale up your career, switch industries, launch a business, refine a skill, or find a new home. Whatever your goal, the Five P's of Success will give you a framework you can follow to get there.

Excel in place first

If you want to move laterally or achieve success in your existing role, you must excel in your current position by gaining more experience and recognition as a subject-matter expert. In your current role, be the best you can be so that higher-ups recognize your ongoing contributions, instead of someone who has gone stale and needs to be replaced.

Maybe you don't want a promotion or a bigger house. You may be happy in the role you have and want to strengthen your leadership skills. Perhaps you don't want to take on more responsibility; instead, you are looking for fresh challenges. Have you decided to generate an additional revenue stream or start your own business? What about staying in your industry, but changing divisions?

No matter what your motivation, you will need to remain nimble and open to change. According to Infinite CXO, "Recent studies reveal that 78% of hard skills will become obsolete within five years." And *Forbes* asserts *half* of all skills will become obsolete within the next year. According to the Institute for the Future, 85 percent of the jobs that will exist in 2030 have yet to be invented.

Let's say you want to stay on the finance team at your organization because you really love what you are doing—or want to remain where you are while you finish graduate school. Maybe you want to keep the status quo so you have more bandwidth to enjoy your family and give them the time and commitment they deserve. How can you show up as the best version of yourself? One way would be to set a goal to increase your annual review rating from a three- or four-point score to the top five-out-of-five score. Employing The Career Ninja Mindset® will get you there. Scoring well on your annual review will ensure pay raises and put you on track for advancement if you desire it later.

If I were running a Career Ninja school, my curriculum would be ...

The Five P's to Achieving Success

1. Follow your PASSION.
2. Make a PLAN.
3. Learn to PRIORITIZE.
4. Have PATIENCE.
5. Be PERSISTENT.

Incorporating the Five P's will build your courage and ignite your ability to take action, so you can be successful at whatever you want to accomplish. By using them, you will learn to cultivate resilience and adaptability in the face of challenges. Your success will not be yours alone, because it will inspire others to accept opportunities that lead them to thrive and grow.

What does the process look like?

In order to be ready for a career transition, you can prepare by using the Five P's. Working through the process will also help you identify where you find fulfillment other than monetary.

Begin by allowing yourself to explore your PASSIONS. Is there a passion project you want to devote more time to? Is there a skill you've always wanted to explore or learn?

You must make a PLAN to stay engaged with your interests and reach your goals, and the research you do will fuel your plan.

You will learn to PRIORITIZE the new things you want to explore. Other people may make demands on what they see as your free time. Identifying your priorities will keep you from putting off the things you enjoy out of a misplaced sense of obligation.

Remember the importance of PATIENCE while adapting to a different lifestyle and schedule that comes with your Ninja Mindset. Don't get frustrated by the lack of change or momentum. When change occurs, it can take time to feel a new sense of purpose and value.

Be PERSISTENT. You may not hit your stride in the first few months or even a year. Keep exploring new activities, including things that are not career focused. Many people find that becoming a volunteer or mentor is a very fulfilling way to share their knowledge and feel valued.

CHAPTER 3

IT'S NOT ALL BUSINESS

Looking back on my career transitions, I recognized they happened hand in hand with personal transitions. My career moves required me to travel quite a bit and even move to a new city. I tested and strengthened my relationships. And with each move, I learned something about myself and gained confidence. Every major life change has an emotional component. Preparing for the emotional impact helps us navigate change. It isn't uncommon if today's enthusiasm over a new position turns into tomorrow's stress and doubt about job performance. Don't let a sudden change in attitude throw you off course. All your emotions are valid and help you examine your goals.

Far too often, we try to separate our personal and professional lives, yet we can function seamlessly and with far less stress when we recognize there will be crossover. We can plan for it and deal with it gracefully when it occurs.

Never say never

My family has lived in New York City since 1967, when my grandmother immigrated to the United States from South America with two young children. She worked as a nurse, and within three years of her arrival, had saved enough to buy a house. I am so fortunate to have her as a strong and positive role model.

I lived upstate when I was a child and spent plenty of time in the city visiting family. Then I moved to the city in 2006 and have spent my adult life here. It is no exaggeration to say I know my town by heart—where to get the best Chinese food at ten at night, how to find discount theater tickets, the best streets to get uptown at four in the afternoon. (OK, none of them really.) I have friends here. I am loyal to my favorite coffee shop. In January 2019, I told my boyfriend at the time I would never leave New York. Why should I? If I wanted a career change, there were plenty of opportunities in the city.

Three months later, a manager's role at my existing company opened up in Chicago. The job was more than a promotion that came with a pay raise. It also came with the opportunity and challenge build a team of customer success managers and a new department from the ground up in a new office. As a bonus, the company would pay all my moving expenses. I never expected it, but this offer was tempting enough to lure me out of New York. I thought, *Let me just send in an application and see what happens.*

I'll tell you what happened: I got the job! I said goodbye to my boyfriend (the relationship had reached its natural conclusion, anyway) and told my friends I'd keep them posted on social media. The Career Ninja Mindset® came into serious play while navigating my departure from New York and my assimilation into Chicago, which was a personal and professional challenge for me. I had a new job and a new city to learn. We'll talk later about tiptoeing through the cultural land mine of pizza.

I had followed my passion by applying for a job that really captured my attention. I made a plan for everything I needed to do once I got the job. I prioritized all of my to-dos. I was patient with myself and others when my plans hit the inevitable snag here and there. The move to Chicago didn't happen overnight; it was a months-long process that required patience. But my persistence in making this major move paid off with a rewarding new experience.

Finding fulfillment

My move to Chicago wasn't only about a pay raise or a new job. The challenge of creating a new department from scratch excited me and gave me the opportunity to put my existing skills to work and learn new ones. It was fun to explore another major city, and I developed new friendships along the way. It was a joyful transition, and I hope this book inspires you to develop the bravery to make your own joyful transitions and find fulfillment in your own life.

The path to fulfillment is not always straight

My neighbor Regina made some surprising decisions that ultimately brought *her* fulfillment. Regina had built a successful career in the tech industry. Like so many others, she enjoyed transitioning into working virtually. But two years in, she lost her husband, and the solitude of working from home was making it difficult for her to deal with her grief. The days seemed longer, and the house seemed too big and empty without John.

One evening while shopping at a high-end cosmetics store, she struck up a conversation with a friendly sales consultant. The consultant expressed how much she enjoyed her job and appreciated that the cosmetic company provided all the training she needed to understand the proper way to use the products. Regina really enjoyed the friendly exchange and noticed how happy the associate was with the job.

Regina thought to herself, *I could do that.* This was a completely different sort of income-earning opportunity that would put her in a position to interact with other people in person, and it required no previous experience.

Regina applied and landed a sales position with the cosmetic company. She completed her training and began as a part-time beauty consultant. Now she had something to look forward to a few nights a week. After she shut down her computer for the day, she traded her sweatpants for a new, sleek black wardrobe, and headed off to her part-time job. The hours she spent at the store flew by while Regina smiled and chatted with the customers.

Within a few months, Regina's sales skills got her noticed, and they offered her of a full-time leadership position. She had a decision to make: Should she give up the seventeen-year tech career that aligned with her college degree? After all, she had reached a high level of accomplishment and had garnered respect in her field. The cosmetic job had a lower base salary but offered commission. She had to be honest with herself—since starting her retail job, she was happier. She was making friends with her coworkers and felt a sense of belonging. Plus, making her customers feel good about themselves gave her a sense of fulfillment she never felt in the emotionally detached tech world.

Regina trusted her instincts and focused on what made her happy, not on how her choices might appear to others. After all, who goes from tech to retail? She bravely stepped away from the tech industry to become a full-time beauty consultant. They promoted Regina to regional manager, and she is now earning way more than she was making at her tech job. She continues to meet more people as she travels to the six other locations in her territory.

Now when we see each other on our evening walks, the look of joy on her face says it all. Switching industries fulfilled Regina's need for camaraderie.

CHAPTER 4

WHAT DOES IT MEAN
TO FOLLOW YOUR PASSION?

Let's say you're a dedicated Chicago Bears fan. You've covered your basement walls with framed tickets, jerseys, and a cocktail napkin signed by Dick Butkus. You were inconsolable after the Colts beat them in the 2007 Super Bowl, even though Prince arguably put on the best half-time performance ever. Some would call you a passionate Bears fan, and you would proudly admit it.

We hear it all the time: "Follow your passion." But what does that really mean? Does that mean you should audition to be an NFL commentator? Should you open an online sports memorabilia store? Maybe. Maybe not.

You will have many passions in your life. They can be wonderful blessings—like winning a triathlon after dedicating yourself to years of daily training. Or you might feel embarrassed about spending over a hundred dollars on the latest trendy item you were passionate about five years ago. If you spend all your money on a temporary obsession and can't afford to pay your bills, your passion has gone too far.

Think of your passion as a dedicated pursuit. When you follow your passion, tempered with discernment and common sense, it can be a useful catalyst. Once you've undertaken a goal, passion can get you through the rough patches, long nights, and unexpected setbacks. Passion can make you a successful entrepreneur, an exceptional employee, and a motivating mentor.

To understand when it is appropriate to harness your passion, consider a less dramatic word—*joy*. Joy seems a little less hazardous, doesn't it? After all, there is no "crime of joy," but many people have gotten into trouble for a "crime of passion." (How many of you are "true crime" fans?)

Passion without discernment can lead to disappointing consequences. Passion alone would not have been enough to justify the steps necessary to make my move from New York to Chicago. My passion for people and travel would not have outweighed low pay, extreme working conditions, or representing a product or company I did not respect. Thankfully, I didn't face any of those issues with the Chicago opportunity. Passion can give you drive, but it can't take the sting out of a poor decision. And passion should never outweigh ethics.

Joy is a feeling. It's the feeling you have when you realize you're smiling. It's silly. It's sweet. It's not always logical. It's the happiness you get from cooking your favorite dish for your friends and family. You don't seek joy the way some people chase happiness. It's a realization. You recognize joy at the moment and upon reflection.

What brings *you* joy?

To find what sparks your joy, take a moment and bring to mind those things for which you are grateful.

Begin with where you are sitting at this moment. Look around you. Do you have somewhere to live? Are you at your place of employment? Do you have a lovely view? How do you feel? Are you healthy? Well-fed? Do you have a family or a pet who loves you? Do you have clean drinking water? Do you have friends or family who support you? Are you employable? Even if you cannot answer *yes* to all of these questions, you still have many things in your life for which to be grateful, and those things can certainly bring you joy.

Between four thousand and ten thousand messages a day bombard us, and they are all designed to make us feel bad about ourselves. It's a concept that's taught in marketing class: "Look for your potential customers' pain points." We receive ads for things we don't need on social media, and habitually watch negative news stories designed to stoke fear and garner ratings. Advertisers profit from selling us drugs or products for problems we never heard of. *Who knew fleshy earlobes were unattractive? I better do something about that.* These constant negative influences do not encourage us to appreciate what we have, just to yearn for what we don't.

What are you passionate about in your career and your personal life?

Look closely at what you are driven to do and ask yourself: *Am I doing this because it's my dream? Or am I trying to please someone else?* It may surprise you to discover who you are really trying to please. Of course, we're aware of trying to make our parents happy, but what about your supervisor? They may have the best intentions in helping you advance, or they may see your success as a reflection of their own. Are you hesitant to stay where you are happy because you think it makes you look less capable? It is very freeing to consider—just because you are good at something doesn't mean you always have to do it. If you are an excellent accountant but find no joy in it, do you want to engage in that industry for the next twenty years of your life?

Are you going along to get along? Are you seeking a promotion because it's expected at your workplace? In the academic world and in large corporations, you are expected to advance, which means there can be an enormous amount of pressure to move up. Many times, you are still learning your current role when the wheels of expectation move you forward and you get promoted out of doing what you enjoy. When you stop shooting for something you don't want, it puts you in a position to identify your true desires.

Practicing gratitude will bring you joy by reminding you of all the things that are *going right* for you. Practicing joy reminds you of what you have instead of what you may be lacking. Gratitude is being appreciative that you have a place to live. Joy is soaking up the view from your balcony.

Gratitude is being thankful you have a job in this economy. Joy is the feeling you get when you help your customer solve a problem. Joy is understanding how to harness your passion.

It's good to have goals and dreams but change rarely comes overnight. Instead of living for tomorrow, focusing on joy will help you find something rewarding you can embrace today, right now, at this moment.

Do you go around grumbling about how much you hate your job? Do you wake up miserable every day that you have to go into the office or log in to work? How long will you have that position before you find *everything* to dislike about it? Do you ask yourself, *How long can I stand being in this position before I start looking for a new one*?

When you have reached that point of dissatisfaction with your job, your behavior reflects it. I've watched this happen with my colleagues, and it shows up in numerous and subtle ways. They come in late or join meetings ten minutes after they start. They don't participate as much as they used to. They don't make suggestions that will improve their working environment. They roll their eyes and sigh heavily. When they do comment, it is usually to point out a fault or something negative. They are sick more often. They find reasons to withdraw from the community, the team, the organization.

If you reach the point of burnout, you start to hate everything in your environment. The carpeting is suddenly ugly. Your chair squeaks. The job you once loved now really aggravates you.

You will improve your outlook and opportunities if you take intentional steps to counteract the mundane annoyances, and that starts with recognizing your mood. You may hate the carpet, but it hasn't bothered you before, so let it go. When you feel cranky, make it a point to look for one thing, no matter how small, in your environment that you appreciate.

Dissatisfied people don't work at their optimum levels, and it doesn't go unnoticed. Wouldn't you rather leave on your own terms than have poor performance be the reason you're dismissed? I'm not saying you have to love your job and keep it forever. I *am* saying you should do your best while you are there. Your company deserves it, your colleagues deserve it, and you deserve it. You don't want a temporary attitude to become your permanent reputation.

To get yourself through times when you're dissatisfied, learn to find the little joys in your day. Is there a coworker you particularly like? Look forward to your conversations with them. Is there a cross-functional team you enjoy working with? Is there a place you like to have lunch? Do you appreciate the dental insurance? Do you have a liberal leave policy? Find something every day to appreciate. Instead of waking up with dread, you'll have more energy to start your workday when you pinpoint a moment to look forward to.

Find a way to turn the little aggravations into opportunities. If the person in the cube next to you brings a stinky lunch every day, that is your opportunity to get up and take a walk—something that is much healthier for you and enables you to cross paths with someone who can put a smile on your face. Focus on the little wins. Find joy where you are.

When you focus on a part of your job you like, it will expand your view of opportunities. What do you like about the enjoyable bits that make you want to learn more? Even if you don't take action for a year or two or five, you are learning and laying groundwork for your future success.

You don't need to make a big change, like finding another job and cutting ties. Perhaps there is a different department you would like to join. Do your research. Make it a point to meet people from that department and ask questions about what they do and the qualifications necessary to do it. Make your interest known. You will never get a chance to move if no one is aware of your desire.

Use your imagination and create a new opportunity for yourself. If there is not another position available for you, design one that engages your interests and talents. Do you enjoy mentoring the new hires, taking them under your wing, and showing them the ropes? Sharing your knowledge helps the newcomers and can be gratifying for you. Is there a task your company outsources that you have the experience to do? Maybe it's research or writing. Step forward and let management know you have the skills. This is an example of an adjacent opportunity within your current company. If there is no raise or promotion in sight, make the most out of the opportunities you have in the here and now.

Your knowledge and connections can be assets in a different industry. Look for a common thread between your current company and a potential employer. For instance, if you repair gaming equipment, you can use those same abilities in medical equipment sales or service.

If you love film and editing, you don't need to move to Hollywood. PR agencies and law firms hire videographers. Wedding planners, real estate agents, and home inspection and repair companies hire drone photographers. Videotapes need editing, and photographers frequently need that service.

You can take almost any skill and turn it into an online course for an additional revenue stream. Are you an Excel wiz? An SEO expert? A marketing maven? You do not need to have decades of experience, just enough to train a beginner.

When you are in a state of dissatisfaction or burnout, make a list of *all* your skills, not just the ones you currently use. You will quickly see how much you have to offer.

CHAPTER 5

BE A STAR IN
YOUR OWN PRODUCTION

Eva always loved the spotlight—beginning when she was four years old, putting on plays for her little brother in the living room—and continued when she tried out for and won several roles in her high school plays. She followed her passion and enrolled as a theater major in college. After graduating, acting jobs were very competitive, so she took a job in corporate communications to support herself and wound up sitting in a cubicle all day writing instruction manuals.

When her company decided to make how-to videos for their clients, Eva stepped up and volunteered to be the spokesperson. After all, who knew the products better? She overcame her hesitation about being rejected or laughed at. If she could stand up on a stage, she could stand up in the boss' office and pitch her idea.

Eva made a sample video to convince the marketing department she was comfortable on camera and that her delivery was as professional as the outside contractor they were considering. Eva convinced them to use her for all the company videos. By following her passion, she created a rewarding opportunity for herself and got out of her stifling cubicle. She still pursues her passion by acting in community theater, and her corporate videos are now part of the sizzle reel she uses to apply for more acting gigs. Most importantly, instead of focusing on the dissatisfaction of the mundane work in a cubicle, Eva created a way to find joy in her work.

Out of office

If you have exhausted all the internal potentials, what does your job supply you *outside* your workspace? Does your job enable you to live in a place that's just right for your needs? Do you have a short commute? Can you drive to your place of worship in ten minutes? Do your parents live around the corner and help you with childcare? Has your kiddo become a soccer star since you moved there?

What are the out-of-office perks and benefits your job provides?

My work allows me to spend quality time with my family because my company has an unlimited vacation policy. Prior to working there, this was something I could not comprehend. I did not know it was even a thing. I mean truly unlimited vacation—not six weeks, not eight weeks, not ten weeks.

When my first nephew was seven months old, his daycare closed unexpectedly for the week and my brother and sister-in-law both had to work. They called me to explain the situation, and I was immediately able to take a week off from work and stay with them to act as the nanny. I really enjoyed the quality time with my nephew, and it remains one of my favorite vacations.

Two years later, shortly before they had their second child, I got to play nanny again. They flew off to a tropical island on a babymoon, leaving me in charge. This time my nephew was two and a half years old, potty-trained, and highly mobile. I warmed the bottles, changed the diapers—and I had to do a lot more cleanup this time, but I loved every minute. I hadn't developed The Five P's then, but that experience definitely planted the seeds.

It was necessary to have a PLAN for the day because my nephew was accustomed to eating on a schedule.

I PRIORITIZED his well-being with a long list of daily tasks I needed to perform, beginning with getting him dressed and ending with reading him his favorite bedtime story.

I exercised PATIENCE because little ones require a lot of that—and energy.

I needed to be PERSISTENT with potty training and the bedtime routine.

And PASSION? I loved to find things that entertained him and brought him joy.

When you find joy in the present, you are functioning with a positive attitude. When you focus on the positive, you see more vistas and opportunities to appreciate. Ever notice that when you are in a good mood and enjoying your project, you can go on for hours? And when you are working on a project you don't like, every minute feels like ten? That's because your positive attitude changes your perception of time. Misery, anger, disappointment—all the negative emotions—drain your energy.

When you are energized by a positive attitude, all those things you used to deny yourself, saying, "I just don't have time," suddenly seem within reach. Does your daughter's soccer team need another coach? The commitment is *only* two nights a week. Volunteering at the local charity fun run *only* requires one Saturday morning.

The Mayo Clinic published the following list of health benefits that positive thinking may provide:

- Increased life span
- Lower rates of depression
- Lower levels of distress and pain
- Greater resistance to illnesses
- Better psychological and physical well-being
- Better cardiovascular health and reduced risk of death from cardiovascular disease and stroke

- Reduced risk of death from cancer
- Reduced risk of death from respiratory conditions
- Reduced risk of death from infections
- Better coping skills during hardships and times of stress

When you reduce stress, you sleep better, which leads to improved health. Good health is something else for which you can be grateful. Focusing on the benefits of your current position instead of the negatives will improve your satisfaction level and reduce your stress level.

CHAPTER 6

OUT OF THE FIRE AND INTO THE FRYING PAN

A fter earning his bachelor's degree, my college friend, Malik, graduated from law school. He invested tens of thousands of dollars in his education, and it paid off when a well-known law firm hired him. His parents were proud, and his lucrative future set.

Malik hated almost every day of being a lawyer. He spent more time on billing than he did with his clients. The late hours exhausted him and, as a consequence, had almost no social life. He had devoted years to getting to a position that made him miserable.

To unwind, Malik enjoyed cooking. No takeout for this busy attorney. Preparing his dinner and testing out new recipes helped him unwind. On one of the many evenings he spent alone in his apartment, slumped over a delicious meal, Malik realized he was no longer being true to himself. He dreaded getting up every morning and trudging to the office. While he was researching case law and discussing torts with his colleagues, he was thinking about stopping at the market on the way home to buy fresh cilantro for a new Cuban dish he was going to prepare that night. While he was supposed to be racking up billable hours, he was online searching for recipes. Malik realized he loved food more than the law and began asking himself what he really wanted out of life —a prestigious career or a gratifying vocation?

Malik was ready to make a change, and it wouldn't be an easy one. He enrolled in an eminent culinary school in Vermont, where he spent the next three years studying culinary arts. After earning his degree, he began working in the restaurant business, paying his dues. Unlike the long hours he put in at the law firm, Malik saw purpose in the effort he was applying toward his new career because he was passionate about food. As anyone in the food and beverage industry can tell you, it's not an easy life. Depending on your area of expertise, your days can begin before dawn and not end until two or three in the morning. It's also physically demanding—you're on your feet all day, lifting heavy pans and boxes of produce, working in kitchens hot enough to boil a lobster.

Malik persevered and landed a position working in the kitchen of a well-known upscale hotel. Within a few years, he worked his way up to head chef and then head of catering, managing a staff of nearly two hundred. Malik was happy. Food brought him joy, and, as a result, he stopped walking around like a cranky, overworked old man. He made friends and cracked jokes. One of those new friends became his wife and they have two children together. Malik no longer drags himself into an empty apartment to have dinner alone.

Malik found his joy. If he didn't have a passion for his work, all the effort required to succeed could have caused him to abandon a career that has brought him a rewarding life.

It's OK to talk to yourself

Don't be afraid to ask yourself, *What do I really want?* Say the answer out loud. That makes it stronger than just an unspoken wish, because sometimes we don't believe we deserve that thought in our head. *I'll never be on the sales team. I'll never get to that level. I'll never be the director. I'll never be able to work in that field.* Allow yourself to dream. Imagine yourself living the life you want, working where you want. What does that look like?

What are you doing? Whom are you working with? Where are you living? Today's daydream can be next year's dream career.

Following your passion can be a challenge if you don't get the support you want, need, or expect from your family, friends, or colleagues. If that is the case, look to the other P's so you can move forward. Practice PATIENCE when other people don't understand or approve of your dreams. Make a PLAN to work around the roadblocks others may drop in your path. PRIORITIZE your own needs. You will need to follow your PASSION and PERSIST until you reach your goal.

CHAPTER 7

MAKE A PLAN

You need to know where you are going before you can devise a plan for how you are going to get there. But where to start?

The first step is to create a *contingency* plan—a plan for unforeseen circumstances that may arise while you are working toward your goal. Employment that was once considered secure is no longer guaranteed. Even tenured professors may face uncertainty if their program or department is eliminated.

It is unpleasant to think about losing a position you love—a place where you feel fulfilled and confident. Having a contingency plan in place will allow you to enjoy your current situation because you are better prepared to deal with surprises. You do not actively have to apply for other jobs, but keep an eye on the market, the competition, and the current compensation for your position at other companies. And, of course, keep your résumé up-to-date.

It is much easier to review your résumé every few months than it is to update it completely after years of neglect. Résumé styles continue to change, emphasizing keyword optimization over lengthy descriptions, so look at online samples when you update yours. Even if you apply electronically, you need to have a handy copy to remind you of your qualifications and employment dates as you complete the form.

Keep your online profile up-to-date and be sure to ask for recommendations. The best method to get a recommendation is to offer to exchange them with your cohorts, team members, and even people you have worked with at other companies.

Clean up your online footprint. This means taking a look at your social platforms from the perspective of a new employer or even a new owner if your company is being considered for a buyout.

Because there is more to your life than your career, make plans for those things that enrich you. Have you always dreamed of playing the guitar? Did you have a poster of Jimi Hendrix on your bedroom wall growing up? Make a plan for learning how to play. Have you researched the type of guitar you want and what it costs? Is it something you need to save for? Have you found a tutor or an online class? Answering those questions is the basis of your plan of action. Put dates to those tasks and hold yourself accountable for completing them because your personal life deserves to be prioritized.

Once you have chosen a goal, your next step is intelligence gathering, a key ninja skill. The information you uncover will feed your plan. Start by asking yourself some questions that will help to define your next steps. The questions in this chapter are for inspiration. Some of them may apply to you, while others may not. Create your own list for self-reflection.

- Do I have a clear objective, i.e., do I know exactly where I want to go?
- What does success look like in this area for me?
- What will change for me when I achieve this goal?
- What actions will I need to take to move me closer to my goal?
- Who can help me achieve my goal?
- What have others done to achieve the same or similar goals?

Have you refined your goal? Perhaps, after some thought, you have created a different goal for yourself. Next, uncover what you *don't* know. Start with an internal query, then move to the external. Answering these questions will help you put together a list of what you need to know or do.

- Why do I want this?
- What will life be like if I achieve this?
- Who will be affected if this comes to be?
- Do I need more information to make a decision?
- Do I need a budget?
- Whom do I need to contact?
- Is there someone who will make a final decision regarding my goal?
- Do I need to complete the tasks in my plan in order?
- Can I perform any of these tasks simultaneously?
- Am I fulfilling all the requirements necessary?
- Is there a timeline?

Notice that you can apply both sets of questions equally to your personal life and your professional life.

You should now have a sufficient amount of discovery to get started on your plan. Write down your responses to the questions you posed for yourself. Don't just perform this as a mental exercise. You will come back to this list, so choose a method that you are most likely to commit to consistently. Do you like notebooks, spreadsheets, voice notes, or Word docs? Choose your method and, by committing your list in a visual or audible manner, you are on your way to keeping your word to yourself. Do you have enough self-discipline to hold yourself accountable? If not, find a trusted partner in whom you can confide. A coach or mastermind group can be very helpful.

Set a target date for each item on your list. Record your progress and celebrate each milestone you reach. Keep stakeholders in the loop. If you have sought advice or assistance from someone, let them know how you have implemented their recommendations. People can be very generous with their time and knowledge, but they do not want to feel as if you've ignored their advice.

When you are creating a plan, you don't have to have all the answers right away. Concentrate on the *next* essential step to complete your plan.

Jose's story

My friend's husband, Jose, executed a brilliant example of making a plan.

Jose always had a knack for understanding people. From a young age, he enjoyed figuring out what made his friends tick and how to persuade them. His interests led him to pursue a degree in marketing, with dreams of climbing the corporate ladder and becoming a chief marketing officer (CMO) at a major company.

During his senior year of college, Jose attended a networking event where he met Michelle, a successful marketing executive. Impressed by her career trajectory, Jose asked for her advice on how to achieve similar success. Michelle shared her knowledge and was pleased she could help someone coming up in the business. She soon took on the role of Jose's mentor and her first piece of advice emphasized the importance of having a clear career plan and setting specific goals.

Motivated, Jose sat down to create his career plan. His vision was to become a CMO at a Fortune 500 company within ten years. He set SMART (specific, measurable, achievable, relevant, time-bound) goals to guide his journey:

- **Specific:** Secure an entry-level marketing position at a reputable firm.
- **Measurable:** Achieve at least two promotions within the first five years.
- **Achievable:** Gain experience in different areas of marketing, including digital, content, and brand management.

- **Relevant:** Continuously improve his skills through certifications and professional development.
- **Time-bound:** Become a marketing manager within five years and a CMO within ten years.

Jose landed his first job as a marketing coordinator at a midsize tech company. His first year was all about learning and adapting. He made it a point to become familiar with the company's products, target audience, and marketing strategies. Doesn't this sound a lot like the ninja skill of infiltration? He also took on extra projects to showcase his skills and enthusiasm.

Jose identified key areas for improvement: digital marketing, data analytics, and project management. He enrolled in online courses and earned certifications in Google Analytics and HubSpot.

Jose's strategy involved gaining diverse experiences and building a robust professional network. He mapped out his career moves for the next few years:

- **Years 1–2:** Excel in his current role and learn as much as possible.
- **Years 3–4:** Seek a promotion to marketing specialist or similar role.
- **Year 5:** Transition to a marketing manager role.

He also joined industry associations and attended marketing conferences to network and learn from experts.

Jose's action plan was precise:

- **Daily:** Allocate time for professional development, including reading industry blogs and practicing new skills.
- **Weekly:** Meet with his mentor, Michelle, to discuss progress and seek advice.
- **Monthly:** Attend networking events and conferences.

Jose's hard work paid off when he was promoted to marketing specialist in his third year. He took on more responsibilities, managing small campaigns and collaborating with other departments.

Jose regularly reviewed his career plan with Michelle, who provided valuable feedback. When a digital marketing project he led significantly increased the company's online engagement, it validated his efforts and motivated him further.

To stay inspired, Jose kept a journal of his achievements and challenges. This practice helped him reflect on his growth and adjust his plan as needed.

As Jose aimed for a managerial role, he sought feedback from colleagues and supervisors to identify areas for improvement. He also took on leadership roles in projects to demonstrate his capability.

He expanded his skills by completing a certification in project management, which helped him manage larger campaigns efficiently.

In his fifth year, Jose applied for a marketing manager position at a larger tech firm and got the job. That role allowed him to oversee a team, manage bigger budgets, and develop comprehensive marketing strategies.

Jose continued to build his network, seeking out mentors at his new company and participating in industry forums. He also started mentoring junior colleagues, which helped him refine his leadership skills.

Jose's journey was not without setbacks. A major campaign he led did not perform as expected, but he used that experience to learn and improve. He embraced the feedback and made adjustments to his approach.

Jose achieved a senior marketing director position. His vision of becoming a CMO was closer than ever. He reviewed his career plan and set new goals, aiming to become a vice president of marketing within the next five years.

Jose's commitment to continuous learning and professional growth paid off. He completed an MBA, which equipped him with strategic business insights. His education, combined with his extensive experience, made him a strong candidate for executive roles.

Finally, in his seventh year, Jose was offered the position of CMO at a Fortune 500 company. His journey was marked by careful planning, relentless pursuit of growth, and adaptability.

Jose's story is a testament to the power of a well-crafted career plan. His methodical approach, willingness to learn, and resilience in the face of challenges were key to his success. As a CMO, Jose continues to innovate and inspire, always looking for new ways to push the boundaries of marketing and mentor the next generation of marketers.

Jose's journey highlights that success is not just about reaching the top but continuously striving for excellence and making a meaningful impact along the way.

Since I was in a different part of the country, I interacted with different organizational leaders I wouldn't have otherwise met, altering my career trajectory. Because I was trying to network and get to know as many people as possible, I joined several groups, including our Women's Employees Resource Group. In a leadership role within that group, I performed additional tasks outside of my day job. Completely planning our annual Women's History Month was one of my responsibilities. This meant I had to wear several hats, none of which I had previous experience with.

I needed to execute a precise plan to invite popular female authors to attend and speak at our events. I started by asking myself: *What do I need to know? Whom do I need to reach out to, and what information do I need to provide?* As I learned more, new questions arose. *What is a standard contract? What are the expectations of book publishers? What are the timelines?* These were the things I needed to find out in order to make the event a success.

The number of people I had to coordinate with was staggering, starting with our internal procurement team, which needed to approve every budget item. The minute you see the word "budget," you know there is a multi-tab spreadsheet involved.

Since this event was to feature well-known authors as speakers, it fell to me to negotiate with their publishers. Consequently, I added "contract negotiator" to my new skill set. I then liaised with speakers to share the scheduling aspects. This required the skills of a travel agent.

We were to provide a copy of every author's book to each participant, which meant more negotiations with each publisher. We held the event during the pandemic, so I couldn't buy the books in bulk and place them on a table for easy pickup after the author talks. Instead, I had to secure the address of every participant and forward those to the publishers, who arranged to ship the books individually.

We broadcast the event over Zoom, and I had to make sure there was enough staff to help with all aspects, including connectivity, admitting participants, muting them, and later allowing audio and video access for the Q&A portions.

A Zoom production is very much like a television show. It requires a studio, a stage, lighting, and sound—which requires an AV team. Thankfully, my company had an internal team ready to assist. The very helpful director of AV asked me for a "run of show," which stumped me because I had never heard of that. A run of show is a very detailed timeline used for theatrical productions and weddings. The AV team uses it to cue lighting, turn mics live, run video footage, and a myriad of other things. It has to be very precise, so no one is standing in the dark or shouting into the void.

Who do I need to be in order to put together a run of show? A wedding planner. If they can calmly cope with bridezillas, then a few authors and AV people should be no problem. I put on my wedding planner's hat and discovered a "wedding project planner," which is a book-like calendar that helped me stay organized and create the run of show. I needed to execute it with flawless precision. I had to follow the plan and stay on top of it, and that planner was the perfect tool.

Much like a wedding, we needed a caterer. That meant another contract to be negotiated and approved and another use for the run of show. Caterers need to know what to serve, when to arrive, how long they had to set up, when to serve, when to clear, and how to find the kitchen and loading dock.

With all of these vendors and speakers, I was quickly becoming a transportation specialist, too.

I did this in addition to my new job responsibilities.

I am a procrastinator by nature, but since I was dealing with famous authors and representing my company, I had to do things in a way that was out of my comfort zone. With all the constant follow-up and moving parts, you can see why it was important to remain patient, persistent, and follow the plan. In the end, it was truly exciting to be able to say that I met with some amazing people who have made an impact on the world. One book was about equal pay for women. One author wrote a book about being underrepresented in corporate America. Another wrote about creating a work-life balance. In the end, I would never have done any of this had I not embraced change by moving to Chicago.

Making a plan is a pathway to success for personal goals as well as business goals. How can you apply these techniques to something you dream of accomplishing? Do you dream of owning a home? Do you dream of retiring? Do you dream of moving to another country?

Allow yourself to dream as a first step to creating a plan. In the next chapter, we will address how to prioritize, so your list does not become overwhelming.

CHAPTER 8

LEARN TO PRIORITIZE

I have admitted to being a procrastinator, but thankfully, being a ruthless prioritizer offsets that character trait. What can I say? It's a gift. I've been that way since childhood.

We get about ten inches of snow during a normal winter in New York state, where I grew up, which makes for some pretty cold months. A coal-burning stove, which needed to be kept running 24/7, heated our house. As a young teen, it was my responsibility to take care of the stove every day after school. I couldn't let it go out.

Back when there were still phones attached to the wall, when I got home from school, I would immediately jump on the phone with my girl-friends. We also liked to call into the radio station to make a song request. Our theory was the more of us who called, the greater chance we had of the disc jockey playing our song because he would get tired of hearing from us.

My afternoon phone habits would often distract me, causing me to forget all about the stove. At least once or twice a week, I would let the stove go out. I became very skilled at lighting the stove quickly before my parents got home because my punishment for letting the house get cold would be a loss of my phone privileges—an unthinkable tragedy for a teenager.

To get the stove running, I had to empty the ashes and dump them outside. Then I had to chop wood into kindling to start the fire and put a log on if necessary. No, this was not in the nineteenth century; I'm not that old. A lot of homes in the northeast US still use coal for heat. After getting the fire going, I had to race back outside to shovel coal into a bucket and carry it back into the house. A bucket of coal can weigh about thirty pounds, so this was no simple task. Nursing the fire required a very specific way of putting coal on the wood. If I added it too early, it would choke out the flame and I would have to start over. If I didn't add enough, it wouldn't catch.

In order to do all these things, I had to be very patient and persistent. I needed a plan for how to execute all this within an hour and a half. Sometimes, I would have to use a fan to get the fire started, which would blow coal dust and ash all over the house, which I had to clean up before my parents got home and realized I had let the fire go out.

Keeping that coal stove going taught me I can accomplish any goal when I focus and put my mind to it. If I had understood priorities better, I would have started the stove before I got on the phone, but clearly, I had a teenager's priorities.

If you are serious about reaching your goals, you will need to learn to prioritize. If you are already good at prioritizing, look for ways to prioritize more areas of your life. And if you are not serious about reaching your goals, put this book down right now; you don't need me.

By getting in the habit of asking yourself the following simple key questions, you will stop reacting and start deciding. You will quickly see that prioritizing is a magical time-saver.

- Do I need to do this now?
- When *does* this need to be addressed?
- Can someone else do this?
- Does it need to be done at all?

Think of prioritization as a process of elimination. We instinctively know what is important, yet we allow ourselves to become distracted from doing the things we should in the order we need to do them. Eliminating distractions or needless tasks frees up our time to do the things that help us reach our goal or have fun. Fun is important, too!

Other people distract us.

"Mom! Where is my backpack?"

I call my friend Alli "GPM," which stands for global positioning mom. She can tell her husband where he put his car keys and instinctively knows her daughter left her geography book in her locker. Again. Alli seems to have the magical ability to locate any item anywhere and can instantly yell out its location. "Look under the kitchen table!" She also has the ability to say "no," as in, "I have no idea. Try looking in the garage. I have to make two more calls before the end of the day." Not only can Alli stay on task, but she also saves time and encourages others to take responsibility for themselves. Try adding the word "no" to your lexicon to help you stay on task, and as a bonus, enjoy how much time you save.

"Hey, we're going out for drinks after work.
You should join us."

Oh, you really want this to be a "yes." You like your new work team, and this is a perfect opportunity to do a little bonding. It's flattering that they invited you. You would enjoy blowing off steam and hearing the latest gossip on the upcoming merger. However, you have a big presentation in the boardroom at 9 a.m. You have spent the last month preparing for it. Can you join the team for just one drink and get home at a reasonable hour, so you get enough sleep and show up alert in the morning? Or have you noticed these folks showing up to work after one of their happy hours with their sunglasses on, shuffling into the kitchen for coffee while mumbling something about needing more sleep? The choice is yours.

Prioritizing doesn't always mean eliminating an opportunity. By examining your approach, you will be able to fit more things into your schedule. You can meet your friends or coworkers without drinking to excess. Before mocktails started gaining popularity, I already had a trick up my sleeve: When I was hosting an event or dinner, I always arrived early to meet the staff or vendors to assure the proper setup. I immediately approached the bar staff and preordered my nonalcoholic drink—cranberry juice with seltzer and a twist of lime, served in a martini glass. I also left a tip equal to or greater than what they would have received for an alcoholic beverage. This choice left me relaxed for the evening and sharp for the next day. This early interaction with staff also established who was in charge, and the service I received was always attentive and efficient.

By considering your choices, you can enjoy an evening with friends and still be at the top of your game in the morning.

"I don't know how. Can you do this for me?"

Don't fall into this trap! This is a variation on a childhood ploy. We've all known that kid whose mom told him to do the dishes or sweep the floor and he consistently did such a poor job of it that Mom eventually reassigned the chore to his sister. There are times you genuinely want to do whatever it is or teach someone else how to perform the task. This doesn't mean you need to assume responsibility for it until the end of time. We have this thing called YouTube now, where you can learn everything from how to change a faucet to how to perform surgery. Let the other person gain confidence by learning how to perform whatever task they tried to push off on you.

We distract ourselves.

You go online to check your work email, and a 40 percent off sale email from your favorite retailer distracts you. Next thing you know, you are shopping online and trying to choose one more item, so you qualify for free shipping. That's an hour taken away from completing a task.

According to the *Harvard Business Review*, dealing with email can take up to three hours, or 28 percent of your day. To cope with my inbox and make better use of my time, I adapted methods from David Allen's book *Get Things Done,* and his GTD method. These are the Four D's that work for me.

- **Do it**
- **Delegate it**
- **Deliver it**
- **Delete it**

Do it: If someone has sent you an email with a request you can complete in two to five minutes, do it immediately.

Delegate it: If someone is making a request, you may be able to delegate it. You can tell them nicely to ask someone else or suggest another person who is more qualified. By delegating it, you get it off your plate and clear your emails.

Deliver it: Someone has sent an email request that you can't delegate because it is your responsibility. Create a "Deliver it" folder and move the email there. When do they need it? Create a corresponding action item on your calendar. Answer Susan's question by the end of the day. Fulfill Mike's request by the end of the week. If the requester doesn't give you a deadline, create your own for the task. When you have completed the task, move the email to a separate folder. Avoid overloading your Deliver it box or you will create stress for yourself and delay reviewing the tasks in the folder.

Delete it. (This also includes File it.) You receive information. Perhaps there is a new log-in procedure for an online system you use. You do not need to take any immediate action, but you may need to refer to this email at some time. File it. If the email does not require action and does not need to be archived, delete it immediately.

Keeping your email boxes clean and freed up helps prevent feelings of overwhelm. I zero out my inbox every day.

Text messages are another major distraction, and you must learn to respond to them in the order of importance. If you are getting ready to join an online meeting, it is common to check texts to make sure no one is having problems logging in. However, refrain from instantly responding to a text that can wait until the meeting has concluded. Showing up late to a meeting is a waste of everyone's time and leaves an especially negative impression, especially if you are the host of the meeting. It telegraphs, *I am more important than you* to all the participants, or *I didn't read Alexis's chapter on how to prioritize.*

I Don't Wanna.

There are four items on your to-do list for the day. One of them is returning a phone call to a client you are certain has something to complain about. All day, you tell yourself, *I'll get to it after I do this next thing.* You think about that call at least twenty times. You keep moving the call lower on your list and even add a few items that don't really need to be done that day. You spend six hours feeling cranky and stressed out. When you finally call the client, it turns out they just wanted to ask you to bid on another job and the entire call takes less than five minutes.

Write the uncomfortable email. We often overestimate the time it takes to complete a task. I can spend hours or days thinking about an email I want to avoid, and when I finally make myself write it, it only takes six minutes.

If you recognize you are guilty of putting things off, I highly recommend reading Brian Tracy's book *Eat That Frog! 21 Great Ways to Stop Procrastinating and Get More Done in Less Time.* Tracy's theory is based on the Mark Twain quote (which I choose to believe is accurate for the sake of the story—and Tracy's book sales), "Eat a live frog first thing in the morning and nothing worse will happen to you the rest of the day."

If you just made a "Ooh, gross!" face, know that I did, too, the first time I came across the book. Tracy posits, "'Eat that frog,' is another way of saying that if you have two important tasks before you, start with the biggest, hardest, and most important task first."

This goes for your personal life as well. Do the chore you dislike the most first. Is it the laundry? I hate doing laundry, so I put it off. I will clean the bathroom, mop the floors, do the dishes, then I'm exhausted by the end of the day and still haven't done the laundry. Tracy's theory is that getting the onerous task out of the way first will give you energy and change your outlook on the day. You will be proud of yourself for finishing a loathsome task and you won't waste your emotional energy on four hours of dread and guilt.

The Association for Psychological Science should conduct a study on how many Amazon packages that we intend to return get shoved to the back of the hall closet or left in the car's trunk until the "return by" date expires. This is money wasted, yet we find a dozen excuses to not drop off the package: *I don't want to fill out the form. I don't want to drive over there. I don't have the QR code in my phone. The parking lot is crowded. I don't want to wait in line. I'd rather do the laundry.* Of course, we could just keep all the wrong-sized clothing and ugly curtains and never have to buy another Secret Santa present, but odds are, the packages will remain shoved in the back of the closet for another year. So go on; return the package. It's money in your pocket.

By getting the onerous chores out of the way first, you can experience a sense of accomplishment and relief. You can prioritize time, expense, and self-care. Learning how to prioritize—when to say no and when to say yes—can help communication within your family, too. When we are in close contact with other people, we may not realize how much we've already asked of them or how much they expect from us.

Make sure you are responding to demands on your time with reasoned logic and are not jumping in to rescue someone who has issued an emotional request. You may have heard the expression "Poor planning on your part does not constitute an emergency on my part." By being clear on what you are willing to do and when you are willing to do it, you manage everyone's expectations.

When you learn to prioritize, you are adopting a healthy habit. You can achieve the work-life balance everyone is always shooting for. The reward is how good you feel when your stress level drops or completely disappears. You can slow down your frenetic pace and feel comfortable scheduling lunch with a friend.

If trying to figure out how to prioritize (and millions of people are but may not admit it) still challenges you, this is a perfect area to work on with an organizational or accountability coach.

Ruthless prioritizing is self-care

When you make work more important than going to the dentist or going for your annual physical, you are practicing martyrdom, not prioritization. How many people do you know who took their health for granted, didn't make time for the gym, grabbed fast food, and then, one day, they're forty-two years old and wondering why they have high blood pressure and cholesterol?

If you don't prioritize your own health, you risk waiting until it's an emergency, and then everything else is going to crash. That one-hour doctor's appointment you missed turns into a six-week recovery from an injury or illness. How is that going to impact your job or the things you enjoy doing? Maintaining your well-being increases your productivity and your quality of life. You must prioritize it.

Make time in your work schedule for your furry family member, too—for their vet appointments and daily routine. Does it make your blood boil if someone says, "It's just a dog" or "It's just a cat?" Our pets are very important family members. They listen to us without comment and are always there to support us when we have had a rough day. They depend on us for everything. If you don't treat them with priority, your work family won't see them that way either. They aren't called "emotional support pets" for nothing.

Once you become a Priority Ninja you will be healthier, more productive, and calmer.

CHAPTER 9

DISCOVER THE BEAUTY
AND POWER OF "NO"

Exercising the power of "no" does not mean being rude to other people. Once you become a Ninja Master of No, other people won't even realize you've said "no." If you are a people pleaser, or timid, or are on the weak side of a power balance, you may fear saying "no."

I am so good at saying "no," I even taught a class on how to do it when I was a corporate trainer. I suggest you begin by changing your attitude. Don't think of it as saying "no"; instead, regard it as speaking your truth. You are being truthful when you say, "I am working on these three projects, and I cannot take on another one." That is the truth. It is not a lie. There is no shame in that.

Many people are under the false impression that virtual workers, the self-employed, and stay-at-home parents have all the free time in the world. My friend felt a little bad that she had to turn down a request from her sister to pick up something from the store, but she honestly replied with, "If I don't get my dog her shots this afternoon, then I can't go on vacation because the kennel won't take the dog." Her sister didn't get mad, nothing bad happened, and my friend enjoyed her vacation.

"Hey, can you get that market analysis to me by end of day?"

You want to please your supervisor for several reasons: She has the power to advance your career objectives, you like being seen as a team player, and she is requesting something you know how to do. However, you're already jammed and don't know how you can fit her latest request into your schedule.

Let's use the decision-making questions to deal with this.

- **Do I need to do this now?** You would have to start on it pretty quickly to finish it by the end of the day.

- **When *does* this need to be addressed?** You could ask for an extension. Does your supervisor really need it today or does she just want to mark it off her own to-do list?

- **Can someone else do this?** Elliot can definitely handle this. As a matter of fact, it would give him the opportunity to have management notice his skills.

- **Does it need to be done at all?** Yes; the market analysis is important for creating next quarter's budget.

This is how you say no without saying "no."

"Yes, Stephanie. Of course, that means I'd have to reschedule [Thing #2 and Thing #3]. Do you want to prioritize those for me?"

As Stephanie ponders this, you offer another solution. "Elliot is efficient at market analysis, and I think he has some time in his schedule."

You have accomplished three things: You have shown you are willing. You have shared the spotlight by recommending Elliot. You have placed the decision-making on Stephanie, who also has choices. She can still get what she wants when she wants it, if she, in fact, needs it today. She can re-prioritize what she has already assigned you or choose to give the task to Elliot. Or she can decide she really doesn't need the analysis today and still wants you to complete it by another date. By saying no without saying "no," you have lowered your stress level.

If you really want to take on something asked of you, respond with a time and date that works with your schedule. "I can have that for you tomorrow" or "I can get it to you next week." Do not fall into the trap of overpromising in order to please someone. Give them your true estimate of completion; they don't have to know your reasoning.

Never-Never Land

Some things never need to be done. Learning to recognize those things will add years to your life.

Are you an online shopper? Have you noticed that, following nearly every purchase, you receive a request to fill out an online survey or leave feedback and a positive review? Feedback is very important for retailers and online entrepreneurs. It helps their ratings and molds the direction of their marketing. You are a nice person and want to inform other consumers about your experience—either positive or negative. But doing this can take up a surprising amount of your time. Save your reviews for businesses you really want to support. There are enough people in the world who like to complain; it doesn't have to be you. Save your time. If a company's service or product is that bad, there will be plenty of other people posting about it. You have goals to meet!

How often are you saying "yes" out of habit or courtesy? Do you have the reputation of being the "go-to" person at church or work or in a group you belong to? Have you created expectations you are tired of fulfilling? Did you pick up the mail for your neighbor once and now you have to watch his house and his cat every time he goes on vacation, which is more often than you do, and he expects you to watch a movie with the cat every time you go over?

What are some other things you never *have* to say yes to?

- Joining a club
- Joining a team

- Visiting a charity
- Signing a petition
- Eating lunch out every day

When you do say "yes," reflect on why you are saying it. Is there ego involved? Do you think you can do it better than everyone else? This may very well be true, but think of it this way: By letting someone else take over a responsibility, it gives them the opportunity to learn something new or improve a skill. This is particularly relevant with subordinates. Many managers do not want to relinquish certain tasks because they have a reputation they want to uphold. Do you get a lot of kudos for being the Spreadsheet King? Are you afraid of someone coming after your job? Your hesitancy to delegate could be based on insecurity. You do not want to be irreplaceable because then you run the risk of being *never* replaceable. You won't get the opportunity to move up or move on because you are too valuable where you are. Position yourself for advancement by being ready to ease out of your role when an interesting offer comes your way.

Do you say "yes" because you want the opportunity to have things your way—like joining the Home Owners Association board so you can exert power over your neighbor's tacky landscaping?

Assess the responsibilities you have assumed. Do you enjoy them? What would you do with that time if you turned the reins over to someone else?

Once you start putting some of these suggestions into practice, you will notice that prioritization also saves time. Are there other ways you can save time? To help you decide, you must first know what your time is worth. There are online calculators, if you need help arriving at this figure, but you can start with using the hourly rate you earn or charge for your services.

Before making a commitment, research how much time it will take. You may be a DIY-er and enjoy doing things around the house, like painting or repairs. Maybe you are fortunate enough to have had a family member or friend teach you valuable life skills that saved a lot of money when you were first starting out—like how to install a light fixture or replace the air filter in your car.

How long does it take you to do it? If a handyman/woman charges less per hour than you make or bill, turn the job over to them. You can earn money while they work. You know every home repair task requires (some cussing) and at least two trips to the hardware store, where you will be tempted to buy the newest power tool.

When money is not a deciding factor, consider the stress you will avoid by turning the task over to someone else. Do you absolutely dread doing your own taxes and subsequently put them off to the last minute? Even if the accountant charges more than your hourly rate, she's faster and you don't have to pop antacids while you search for the correct forms.

Things you may want to turn over to others:

Car washing
Grocery shopping
Home repair
Laundry
Landscaping
Coding
Web design
Graphic design
Email management
Writing
Scheduling
Bookkeeping
Travel arrangements
Cleaning

If it doesn't save you money or reduce your stress, there's still one more thing to consider—leisure time. That's the time you get to enjoy while someone else is performing the tasks you have delegated. You can take the kids to the pool, then return to a house you didn't have to clean. You can come home from a long day at the office to a delicious, hot meal that was delivered to your door. You get to put your feet up, pour a beverage of your choice, and relax.

CHAPTER 10

LORD, GIVE ME PATIENCE

"Lord, give me patience." Have you ever heard anyone say that? It's the type of thing uttered by a grandmother with her eyes closed, as she shakes her head slowly from side to side. She could be referring to an encounter with an incorrigible grandchild, a grocery store clerk who can't make change, or the cable guy who insists the outage is somehow her fault. By the time you have lived long enough to be the age of a grandmother, life has taught you not only that patience is a virtue, but that it's also a useful tool to cope with setbacks and aggravations.

The Japanese culture reveres their ancestors and, therefore, honors their wisdom. It's reasonable to assume that the wisdom of prior generations would be incorporated into the ninja's collection of tools. Our elders haven't necessarily slowed down because they have bad knees. They have learned the wisdom of patience, which slows one's pace. Patience is taking the time to pause and reflect and allow space. Patience is an essential ninja skill used for infiltration and assimilation into the enemy camp, adapting to the culture, and building trust among the staff. The stories of famous ninjas tell us that some of them spent years undercover, collecting intel.

The modern world is largely a culture of busyness and speed, with terms like *hustle*, *grind*, and *crushing it* sprinkled into the lexicon to normalize the frenetic pace. We have entertainment on demand, same-day delivery, and instant messaging. Developers release more than 2,500 apps every day. Update your programs. Refresh your screen. Buy the upgrade. The world is whizzing past. Who has patience anymore?

In this chapter, we will explore the value and ninja skill of patience. Take a breath. Close your open tabs. Give yourself permission to slow down.

As you read through the previous chapters, you may have found yourself saying "I know that" or "Alexis is right; I ought to do that." Some of what I have written here is obvious. You already know these things. So, why am I repeating them? Because you haven't taken action yet.

Now, don't beat yourself up about that. Everyone is guilty and we all benefit from well-meaning reminders. That's why we work with coaches or mentors. Although they aren't always profound or reading from the latest industry journals, they provide us with guidance and the opportunity to hear the truth coming from another source. This is why you read more than one book on a topic, because each one offers a different perspective. Four people can present the same topic, and each one offers a fresh viewpoint or communicates in a unique style. The way you identify with a speaker, author, or teacher also impacts the way you will receive their message. Or perhaps you've heard the same thing for years but are only now in a frame of mind to receive a message that will change your life for the better. A mother can tell her child six times, "Don't hang out over there," but cool Uncle Jack says it once, and suddenly it's obeyed as if the request is reasonable.

I am reminding you to leverage skills that are within your reach. Patience is one such skill, and it requires practice to become part of your natural way of being.

Begin by developing patience with yourself. This means giving yourself grace at every opportunity. Grace has many connotations, and "mercy" and "compassion" are among them. Grace is not based on merit. You don't have to earn it or feel you deserve it.

If you didn't get the promotion you wanted and worked so hard to win, give yourself grace. You have gained something from the effort you put into applying for it. Perhaps you have learned a new skill or made new connections that will benefit you when the next opportunity arises.

Is it taking you longer to get your degree than you planned? Give yourself grace. Are you trying to carry eighteen credits and work full-time? Are you taking care of a family member while you are going to school? Yes, you are eager to get your degree, but at what price? Your health? Your relationships? What is the worst thing that will happen if you need another semester or another decade? Look at your objectives and prioritize, then practice patience.

Learning new things is inevitable. In the past month alone, I bet you have had to learn at least three new ways of doing something. Did you have a digital lock installed on your front door? Is there a new team communication platform at work or a client management system? Do you have a new oven with Bluetooth capability to connect to your phone, and now you have to learn how to use it?

Even when we are not learning new technology, we are learning new processes. The process for something as common as getting a driver's license differs from state to state. There are new procedures to learn at your university and certainly at a new company. Even recycling rules differ from neighborhood to neighborhood and year to year. Separate it. Don't separate it. I still have guilt about all the plastic rings I recycled before I learned you were supposed to cut them up. I did not know they wound up impacting wildlife.

You will become more patient by creating realistic expectations. Make the time and take the time. A company's lexicon is a perfect example. Have you ever started a new job, bravely walked into your first meeting, and sat there wondering if the attendees were speaking a different language? There are acronyms for this and initialisms for that. You thought CTV meant Canadian Television, but Brenda is talking about *connected* television, and clearly she doesn't mean screwing the cable into the wall.

Whether you are going to work for a company or pitching to them as a client, read their website and monitor the firm's social media posts to become familiar with the terms they use—before you walk in the door, whether that is physically or virtually. Some terms are used only internally. Make a note of them. Often, you can pick up the meaning with contextual clues. Otherwise, find someone to ask. One day that someone may be you and you will remember how lost you were at first.

We learn a lot about company culture and interpersonal relationships while sitting around the conference table or joining an online conference call. You may be eager to show what a team player you are and prove yourself by jumping in with twenty suggestions and five new strategies. Just slow your roll there, friend. Often misquoted but always true: *It is better to remain silent and be thought a fool, than to open your mouth and remove all doubt.* (Possibly a quote by Maurice Switzer, published in1907.)

If you are an introvert by nature, it won't be difficult for you to remain silent during a meeting. For enthusiastic personalities (Enneagram Type 7, the Enthusiast, or Type 8, the Asserter; Myers Briggs "E" Extrovert; Human Design Manifestors) it will be good practice for you to take on the role of observer; there is so much to learn.

When you are not waiting for a lull in the conversation to jump in with your brilliant ideas, it gives you time to look and listen. Begin by noticing body language. Who is paying attention and engaged? Who is taking notes? Who is distracted? Who has arrived late? Are the participants looking at one another? Are two specific participants interacting directly with each other and excluding the group? In which direction are their bodies turned? Are their arms crossed? You can tell a lot about interest levels and alliances by watching for these clues.

There are countless books written about body language and nonverbal cues. Understanding unspoken communication will go a long way in helping you decipher what other people think and intend.

Next, listen not only to what people are saying, but how they are saying it. Who makes supportive statements? Who thanks their team members and shares praise? Who offers solid suggestions? Who offers research? Who offers a long-term perspective?

Does Val smile while she is disagreeing with a statement or saying something negative? Beware the person who begins a statement with

"No offense" or "I just wanted to let you know." They know full well they are being unkind and just do not want to take responsibility for their actions. They do not want to be called out for their bad behavior.

Whose behavior is bothering you, turning you off, or offending you? You can learn valuable lessons from these people. This is *not* how you want to behave or have others perceive you.

Even though you are experimenting with the role of the observer, you still need to be prepared when you attend the meetings. If you are called upon to present, have all of your data ready.

Take notes. When it is your turn to speak, make informed comments based on what you have learned. You may decide to eliminate some points from your presentation or expand on ideas that were presented while you were an observer.

Ask questions. By listening to gather information instead of listening for the opportunity to jump in with an opinion, your mind has time to process the info. Ask for clarifications and additional details so you fully understand the context of what is being said. Your questions give others an opportunity to add information or identify gaps in their presentations.

Patience is also important when you are already in a leadership position. I read a recent study that showed when leaders stopped attending team meetings, the team was able to come up with better strategies faster. They weren't constantly seeking validation in every microexpression of their leader. *Do they agree? Do they think this idea is stupid? I have an idea, but I don't want to say it because I don't want Maria to think I'm an idiot.*

Without the distraction of leadership, their ideas, either genius or imperfect, can be freely expressed and can spark inspiration in another team member.

As a leader, it will take patience to trust your team and wait for the results. Be patient enough to wait and see what your team comes up with before you decide on how to move forward on a project or accomplish a goal. Let your team devise strategies instead of solving problems for them. This is one of the things I incorporate when I coach my team, and it is an important part of coaching anyone at any age—letting them come up with their own solutions. That means giving them the space and time to share their thoughts. If you are on a team and you want to be successful, you don't always have to give the answer or be the smartest person in the room. If you practice patience, you might hear other ideas that spark a thought, an inspiration, or a solution, which, when shared, will allow you to shine.

Patience does not need to be for a day or a week or even an hour. Patience can be holding your tongue for as little as six whole minutes.

Patience and grace can mean slowing down to treat others with compassion. Make it a habit to question someone's behavior instead of giving a knee-jerk response. I don't mean asking, "What on earth is wrong with you?" Although you may think that. Take the time to consider what may be going on in their life that you don't know about.

Did someone turn you down? Were they mean to you? Ignore you? Chances are their behavior has nothing to do with you. They are having a bad day. They are ill. They are exhausted or depressed. Do not let your first thought be that they woke up that morning and decided to make your life miserable for their own amusement. When you are patient with others, it fosters clear communication. Instead of responding with equal brusqueness or bad humor, consider giving the other person options.

"Would you like to come back to this later?"

"Is there someone else I should be talking to?"

Responding with "I understand" can take the other person by surprise and temper their aggression.

You won't always encounter rude behavior. You may have to practice patience with someone else's enthusiasm or exuberance, like when a new employee's eagerness grates on your nerves.

Your calm reaction to any situation allows the other person to take a step back, perhaps recognize their behavior, and start again. They may even offer an explanation. "Sorry. I was up all night with our newborn." "Did you see the game last night? The Ravens won in overtime."

And sometimes, people are just jerks. Move on.

Other people may not have patience with you either. They expect you to learn your lessons sooner, grow up faster, and see things their way. Immediately.

How do you react when your parent, partner, friend, or teammate does not understand or approve of your dream? Do you *need* their approval? Do you walk away from your goal? Do you need to win them over? It is very easy to become excited by an inspiration, and that is useful energy to propel you forward. However, the ideas that are fully blown, achievable, and realistic in your mind do not necessarily appear that way when you express them out loud.

If you announce "I'm moving to a remote island in the Mediterranean!" your grandmother may immediately begin praying for you and your brother may ask for your car.

It may take a little patience to explain that you've received a job offer, have a friend who lives there, are considering relocating temporarily, or are leading a top secret training retreat for the government. The people around you may need a few more details in order to feel comfortable with, or at least understand, your decision and enthusiasm. You will also need patience to listen to their concerns. They may think you are crazy but could bring up some very good ideas you might want to consider. Asking for opinions or help can gain their buy-in and eventual acceptance of your plan. Remember, you do not have to take their advice. Have a bit of patience with yourself and consider incorporating more steps to make your dream a reality. Or you may decide you are not really cut out to live on a remote island once you find out there are no Starbucks there.

Have you ever driven through Atlanta?

Having patience with our families and the key players in our life is always important in maintaining strong, healthy relationships. My friend Deanna's parents were flying to Atlanta for a wedding. She convinced them that using a rideshare service was a safer and more efficient option than renting a car at the airport. Have you ever driven through Atlanta? The road system there makes the Indy 500 look like a Sunday drive. Deanna patiently answered all their questions, researched the car rental fees, and compared them to the approximate cost of using a rideshare service for the weekend. When she mentioned that Interstate 285 is rated the deadliest highway in the United States, she convinced her parents to leave the driving to someone else.

Next, Deanna showed them how to download the rideshare app on their phones and how to use it. Although Deanna offered to do a test-drive with them before they left for Atlanta, her parents declined, saying that it would be a complete waste of money.

Deanna dropped her parents at the airport and felt much better about their trip. She didn't even mind when her mother called the next day to tell her about how they were a little worried when the driver showed up at their hotel. He didn't seem old enough to have a driver's license, but she admitted that he was a nice young man, working his way through college. He was also engaged to a girl from Tennessee and missed his golden retriever, Rocky, who stayed home with his parents.

Patience gave Deanna peace of mind, and her parents now use a rideshare service every time they want to go "into town" for dinner. "The traffic is awful, and the parking is worse. We like getting dropped right at the door," her father told her.

If you extend more patience in your world, it will have a positive impact on others, your relationships, and your brand (the consistent way you appear to the public). This includes not getting frustrated with a coworker who doesn't pull their weight. Avoid the temptation to complain. "Ugh, Janet. There she goes again, pretending to work. She doesn't do her part of the project. I have to cover for her all the time. It's just a pain in the neck."

What patience and grace are you giving to Janet? Did you know that one of her family members has cancer? You don't know what other people are going through. You don't know what kind of terrible situation they could be in. Practice applying patience to as many situations as you can.

Always start with patience—and understanding, when appropriate. Dig a little deeper before making snap judgments and catty comments. Sometimes, this is difficult to do without intruding on someone's privacy. It is their story to tell. Consider there *may be* a story. Perhaps they are working a second job because their spouse lost theirs. They may be working a night shift somewhere else, making it admirable that they can show up on time for their day job. No wonder they're exhausted and not delivering up to their ability—or *your* expectations. Some people are in a place in their lives when they are raising their children *and* are responsible for their parents. That's a lot of work—cooking, cleaning, following up on prescriptions, doctor's appointments, driving car pool.

I am not telling you to excuse poor performance or bad behavior indefinitely. But you may consider observing the situation for a while to see if it is temporary. Then you can take your concerns to your manager, HR, or whatever process is in place at your company.

If you have ever tried to train a new puppy or kitten, you may be able to identify with the need for patience—and carpet cleaner. You will definitely need additional cleaning supplies when you get a puppy or kitten.

How can you apply patience to your career? Patience can help you interact better in the workplace. The people around you will notice and appreciate your calm, measured attitude. Patience includes not instantly expressing your negative opinions. It is easier to trust someone who is not whining and complaining about what so-and-so is doing or not doing. Subconsciously, people will wonder if you talk about them the same way, and this will cause them to avoid you or be closed off in their conversations with you.

We talked about prioritization and your plan; you need patience for those things to come to fruition. You may get frustrated because you didn't get promoted when you thought you should. Step back and remember that, although you may be temporarily delayed, you haven't totally been derailed from your goals. Expressing your frustration will negatively impact your behavior, your attitude, and how you exist in the world. Guard against frustrated behavior that could damage your reputation at your current position. You need to function at an even higher level when you are considering a move. This means monitoring your behavior apart from the work environment when you are on social media. Resist the temptation to take out your frustrations with posts that complain about workplaces, team members, or circumstances.

Remember, potential new employers and supervisors check references and your online footprint. A stellar reputation will follow you throughout your career. You also have no way of knowing if and when you may work with the same people in the future. Leave the best impression you can, no matter what the circumstances or your treatment in your current position. Like Michelle Obama said, "When they go low, we go high."

Impatience, dissatisfaction, and frustration can also leak into your personal relationships. Are your friends tiring of you constantly complaining about your job, how many résumés you've sent out, and statements like, "But that job was perfect for me"? Do you find you have less patience with your family, children, or partner? Maybe they aren't the ones getting on your last nerve. Maybe your impatience is with yourself. "But I'm experienced. I have a degree. I want it. I want it now."

Circumstances are constantly changing. New opportunities arise every day. There is no one perfect job. Jobs are not soulmates. They are temporary conditions that allow you to support yourself. Yet how often do we measure our value by the job we hold? Do you let your title define you? Are you more successful working for a Fortune 500 company or being an entrepreneur? When you do not get a job you were sure was "in the bag," use that opportunity to reflect on why you wanted that position so badly. Often, it is the low-hanging fruit that attracts us. The job that looked like a fast way out of your current workplace. The job that offered a 5 percent salary increase. What are your aggregate goals? Your long-term goals? Would that opportunity have fulfilled them? Perhaps not. Don't be so quick to give up on long-range goals. Do not get frustrated with a lack of change or momentum.

The world goes in cycles. Sometimes companies are hiring rapidly and sometimes there's a slowdown. You may need to do a little research to discover why your job search is taking so long. Is it how you're marketing yourself, the jobs you're looking for, your experience, or how you're going about it?

Getting the perspective of a third party can help you answer those questions. Consider hiring a résumé writer to start. Do you need to consult a coach or mentor to give you broader guidance? You need patience and humility to take feedback and constructive criticism about what you might need to do to change your situation. If you're not patient, you won't be in the mindspace to accept that information.

The solution to a problem could even come to you in a dream. You need to be open to the concept that what you want may not happen right away and that you need to develop the skill of persistence (which we talk about in the next chapter). Are you familiar with the term "Just sleep on it"? That's patience. Be patient with yourself. When you give yourself space, the right decision will come to you.

Circumstances are not the only thing in constant flux

Emotions can change quickly. Have you ever been crying one minute and laughing the next? Have you ever suddenly been angry or sad out of the clear blue sky? Emotions, even the positive ones, can distract and drain us. Recognize that feelings are temporary and do not make major decisions while in a highly emotional state. Waiting for your emotions to come back into balance requires patience.

I suggest learning a technique to help you deal with emotions and stress. Don't roll your eyes at me, expecting me to tell you to meditate. Meditation is not for everyone. I do not expect you to light incense and sit still for an hour on an overpriced pillow you ordered on the internet. *But did you know …* doing dishes or taking a walk can be a form of meditation? "Why is that, oh wise one?" Being focused on a repetitive task takes your mind off the situation that is bothering you.

When you become frustrated with performing a task or looking for an answer, change the scenery. Get up. Do some stretching to get your blood circulating and gently flex your spine. Leave the room. Engage in another activity that gets your body moving.

If you are able to go for a walk, make a game of being as observant as possible. Do you know the names of the trees you pass? Is there a breeze? How is the construction coming along on the new building across the street? What do your shoes sound like on the pavement? Are you in a place where you can go barefoot and feel the soil, sand, or grass under your feet?

When you wash dishes, focus on the water temperature, having the right amount of soap, examining every part of the pan to make sure it is free from caked-on food, rinsing, stacking, drying, and putting it away. This activity can have a calming effect. At the very least, you'll be relieved and have a sense of accomplishment when you finish.

Paying attention while walking or doing the dishes is called "mindfulness meditation" or "insight meditation." Google it for more details on how to practice it and how you can incorporate some form of meditation into your daily life.

Perhaps breathing techniques are more your style. You can do them almost anywhere, and other people won't even notice. Begin by breathing slowly through your nose. Mouth-breathing is associated with panic and the fight-or-flight response, so simply by focusing on breathing slowly through your nose, you can begin to calm and center yourself. Breathe in for a count of four. Hold the breath for a count of four. Exhale through the nose for a count of four. Hold that emptiness for a count of four. And repeat. Just a few rounds of this will slow your heart rate and increase the flow of oxygen to your brain. You could even feel smarter afterward!

If you are way too cranky, fidgety, or frustrated to try any of these techniques, watch something funny or cute on the internet. What's your jam? Do you like comedians? Cute kittens? Silly puppies? Indulge in at least fifteen minutes of mindless videos, and your mood will slowly improve. You're not doomscrolling; you're chill-scrolling.

Our moods and emotions can overtake us suddenly. When we are feeling down, we want to feel better right away. When we are riding high, we want it to last forever. When things aren't going your way, when you are rejected or hurt, it is easy to fall into the trap of thinking you will feel awful forever. I assure you; the passage of time will change your perspective—and that results from patience.

If someone breaks up with you—you may think you'll never find love again. With patience, you may find your true love is just a swipe away. A fresh perspective may show you that your partner wasn't the best match for you, anyway; they were controlling and didn't take you seriously. And on the bright side, you don't have to pretend you actually enjoy watching wrestling or ice skating for four hours straight.

If you lose your job—you may *fear* your reputation is ruined, and you'll be eating food out of a garbage bin by next week. You *will* find another position, and your cat won't necessarily have to share her Tender Vittles with you. The new job may be more rewarding. Patience and perspective will help you see that you might have stayed in your previous position because it was comfortable and felt secure. The process of searching for something new can open your eyes to the fact you had advanced as far as you could.

As you can see from the two scenarios above, it is possible to benefit from situations you do not control. What at first seems like a setback or a tragedy can be an advantage. You learn new things (even about yourself) and align yourself with new opportunities. What you viewed as failure or disappointment can be a catalyst for growth and newfound joy.

When you are mindful of practicing patience, you can more easily manage your expectations. Do not get frustrated if you don't land a new job next week or find the love of your life on your next coffee date.

Patience is a mindset that is closely related to your perception of time. Waiting a day, an hour, or even a few minutes, as opposed to reacting immediately, gives your emotions time to settle. This will give you the opportunity to examine a situation that may have triggered you from a different angle. How many times have you read an email and instantly wanted to type an emotional response?

An hour later, the sender may realize they asked you for something completely unreasonable (because they were reacting and had not read this chapter about patience). In many cases, people shoot off emails without trying to solve a problem themselves. With a bit of patience, they can solve the problem without your input or realize there *is* no problem to solve. I wouldn't necessarily call this procrastination, but sometimes situations have a way of resolving themselves when you don't jump in immediately and try to fix things.

You need patience to build your brand and your reputation at your organization. Pay careful attention to how you are seen, heard, and remembered. How do others perceive you? You can just *show up* or you can choose to *stand out* in a positive way. Building relationships, seeking out one-on-one conversations with other people will have them talking about you (in a good way) when you are not in the room. Wouldn't it be nice to overhear, "Hey, have you seen the work Susan's been doing on Project X and Project Y and how she's been partnering?"

Do not stand by silently and wait to be chosen for the team. Speak up. Ask questions and when you identify needs that align with your skill sets, volunteer to join the project. Become an asset.

It takes time for these opportunities to develop. It requires more effort than simply saying, "I wanna work on the project management team and they should take me because I'm fantastic." Be careful you do not confuse enthusiasm with being qualified.

Imagine yourself as a ninja. Use your observational skills for intelligence gathering and begin with self-assessment.

- Ask yourself if you have the skills, not just the desire. Is there specific information or experience you need to gain in order to reach your goal?

- How have you shown that if you're given the opportunity, you'll be the right person?
- Have you explored the steps necessary to show your value?
- Whom have you talked to in the department or on the team you want to join?

It takes time to build those relationships and be seen as a person who would function well in the role.

Managing your expectations builds patience and comes from doing your homework to uncover the steps you need to take, then prioritizing those steps.

Learn patience by observing others

Is there someone in your life you can look to as an example of patience? For me, it is my mother. She shows me every day that patience is an act of compassion. My mother is retired and still enjoys working as a volunteer tax preparer. As you know, that is very seasonal work, and my parents schedule their lives around tax season accordingly. This includes taking care of my ninety-six-year-old grandmother.

My mother travels to Virginia for a month or two to spend time with my grandmother, and sometimes my grandmother will come to New York for two or three months to stay with my parents. During tax season, my mother's siblings get custody of Gram. Living close to my parents gives me the opportunity to see my grandmother and witness firsthand the care my mother gives her. Gram is sharp as a tack but requires assistance and patience. In addition to the extra cooking, cleaning, and laundry that result from having another person in her home, my mother has to schedule Gram's doctor's appointments, drive her there, and be her health advocate at the appointment. She takes notes to repeat to my grandmother later and shares updates with the other members of our family.

Mealtimes are a challenge. Let's just say Gram knows what she likes and isn't shy about telling you what she won't eat—and that changes daily. Yesterday, she loved vegetables; today she turns her nose up at them. My mother patiently works with my grandmother for every meal to find something she will eat. Being able to chew her food requires Gram to put her teeth in, which she sometimes refuses to do. Because she didn't want to be a bother (despite her fussy and constantly changing dietary requirements) she didn't tell anyone her teeth didn't fit correctly and were causing her pain, so she just stopped putting them in. This was one more thing for my mother to supervise. New, proper-fitting teeth? Check. Happy Gram? Check.

Some days, my mother winds up yelling at my grandmother. Not because she is mad at her, but because Gram doesn't remember where she left her hearing aids.

Many older people take a lot of medications. This is a big responsibility for my mother. She has to count out the pills and create a timetable for taking them. Gram takes some in the morning; others she takes with food. She can't drink grapefruit juice with another. She takes some twice a day.

And through it all, I've never seen my mother lose her patience. What a wonderful role model she is.

In what areas of your life can you practice more patience? At first, you may find this frustrating because it requires practice in the literal sense of the word—a repeated action over time. However, developing this skill is to your benefit as it will improve your outlook, your relationships with others, and prepare you for the next chapter "Persistence."

CHAPTER 11

PERSISTENCE PAYS OFF

Let's contrast patience with persistence. Patience is based on time. Waiting. Waiting to send the email. Waiting to react. Waiting to gain the right experience or collect enough data. Persistence is repetitive. A Japanese proverb describes persistence best: *Fall down seven times; stand up eight.*

Persistence is looking for more than one source of information. Persistence is continuing your search for the right resources that align with your goals. Patience is putting a project or dream aside for a better time. Persistence is coming back to your dream to see it through to completion.

Persistence is essential for problem-solving

Several years ago, I acquired two multifamily rental properties and a laundromat. This seemed like a very solid investment because the houses already had long-term tenants who consistently paid their rent. The laundromat was successful because of its strategic location in a neighborhood that supported the business.

My investment resulted in two years of low-risk success. Then, the real estate bubble burst. Interest rates went through the roof, my mortgages skyrocketed to nine grand a month, and tenant rents weren't covering my expenses. I found myself in an upside-down situation. But that wasn't the worst part. I had convinced my sister to invest with me and she was in the midst of planning her wedding with a budget based on this investment income. My guilt was overwhelming because I had gotten her into a terrible financial situation. How was I going to bail us both out of it?

Working with my executive coach kept me focused and led me to discover a pathway that got me out of a financial mess without declaring bankruptcy or having judgments made against me. And my sister was able to pay for the beautiful wedding of her dreams without skimping on the budget.

Patience was not enough to see me through. Patience alone could have meant sitting alone in a dark corner, meekly waiting for foreclosure. Patience alone could have meant doing nothing while my loans defaulted. Patience alone might have meant enduring the guilt of causing my sister's financial loss. Instead, I used my ninja skill of persistence to get me through those difficult times. I had to be persistent in my belief there was a way out of my situation (faith). I had to be persistent in finding the right people to advise me (discernment).

In order to get out from under that mortgage without going bankrupt and or having judgments against me, I needed to research the options available for someone in my position. I needed to find ways to avoid bankruptcy. I had so many questions. *What would happen if I just walked away? Is there any way to get out of this without ruining my credit?* I found the answers through persistence. I needed to be brave enough to ask the hard questions. I couldn't stay ashamed. I needed to be someone who was not embarrassed to face the truth. I needed to be inquisitive and creative. I needed to be strong enough to ask for help. Read that phrase again: strong enough to ask for help. So often we view asking for help as a weakness, when in reality, it is quite the opposite. Asking for help requires grit to put yourself out there and admit you need assistance.

I reached out to my bank on a fact-finding mission, but it wasn't enough to just gather the information. I had to ask myself a third question: *What do I need to do?*

And what I needed to do was continue working with the bank and follow their process—which was a long and complicated one. During that time, I learned about a deed in lieu of foreclosure. After filling out a lot of paperwork, I was able to come to an agreement with the bank, wherein they essentially took the house back. With a deed in lieu of foreclosure, you don't have to declare bankruptcy. There are no liens or judgments against you, and it doesn't destroy your credit. The deed in lieu also preserved my sister's credit.

That process allowed me to move forward—past the shame and guilt. Initially, I had thought there was no way out. I also felt like I should have known better because I was in the industry. Patience with myself and the bank and persistence in following up with all the paperwork and all the hoops they made me jump through enabled me to get everything I asked for.

Going through the financial recovery felt like a superlong process, but, in reality, it only lasted three or four months. In the end, everything worked out. I was able to be persistent in a terribly tough situation that had me almost paralyzed with fear and guilt. This type of persistence builds resilience—the ability to cope with the unexpected curves life throws you.

Persistence is key to ninja discipline, too. Ninja training is some of the most rigorous in the world. Sometimes, training begins during childhood. Students engage in the daily practice of athletics, martial arts, weaponry, and the techniques of stealth, which endow them with some remarkable skills.

It is said a well-trained ninja can jump seven feet straight into the air. How could they accomplish this? Walking on hot coals? That's certainly one method, but I'm talking about persistence. One theory is that every day, the ninja would jump over a bamboo shoot (the type growing out of the ground, not served on top of your stir-fry). As the shoot grows, the leap into the air must be higher. Depending on the type of bamboo, it could take two to seven years to reach a height of seven feet. Do you think students had to start all over again with a fresh shoot if they fell on it and crushed it?

Luckily, you can practice persistence without having to spend years jumping over bamboo. You need to be continually learning new skills and sharpening your industry expertise. For some companies, continuing education is mandatory and included in your compensation package. Instead of dreading the seminars and workshops your company requires you to attend, be grateful for the free training. Not only will you keep yourself on the internal promotion track, but you are also adding additional bullet points to your résumé should you decide to move to another company.

If your company does not provide training, seek it out. There are endless online courses that provide professional certifications. Additional skills will enable you to move laterally or upward within your own company and give you a competitive edge when applying elsewhere.

It is critical to practice your craft. Accountants need to stay on top of the latest software and regulations. Marketers have to become experts in what's trending in the media. You may not need to master every technology in your field, but you certainly need to be aware of it.

Practice soft skills like interviewing. Since so many interviews are virtual, practice before your appointment. Find the ideal location where you will join the call and test the lighting and microphone. Clean the area so there is nothing distracting in the background and your back is not to a window. Then record yourself speaking into the camera. When you review your recording, watch for any habits or behavior you can eliminate or improve. Do you slump or mumble? Does your attention wander around the room? Interviewers will gauge your engagement and attitude as well as your answers. Even if you aren't interviewing, practicing those skills will ease your comfort level in many other kinds of interactions.

There are many jobs that require client communication skills. Leading a call with a stranger can be very intimidating for some people, especially when they need to make requests or deliver unpleasant news. You can practice this skill and that will enable you to feel more comfortable fairly quickly. Make notes about the points you need to make on the call. Create a script for how you will introduce yourself and how you will end the call. Get a friend or family member to rehearse with you.

Read industry publications to keep track of the competition. Attend conferences to make new connections. Knowledge is power and networks are priceless.

Finding my authentic voice

The lessons I learned about persistence continue to serve me. Recently, a women's leadership conference invited me to speak, and I decided to invest in a speech writer to take my keynote address to the next level. Three thousand dollars wasted.

I had done my due diligence by finding an experienced speech writer, but I didn't know enough about speech writing to ask him the right questions. I gave him my topic and my notes and off he went to write the equivalent of what I thought was sure to parallel Martin Luther King Jr.'s "I Have a Dream" speech or, at the very least, Jim Carrey's commencement speech at Maharishi International University. For three grand, I wanted the speech to be brilliant, inspiring, and… hilarious.

What I got was pompous, cold, arrogant, and… boring. And that's not just my opinion. I read the speech to my family, friends, and coach, and the feedback was consistently bad. "This doesn't sound like you. As a matter of fact, it doesn't sound like something any woman would say."

To paraphrase, the tone of the speech was: *I am fantastic. I do all these great things. You should want to be just like me because I'm a superstar.* All I can say is, thank goodness the people around me don't think that is what I sound like, and they were candid enough to give me honest feedback on the speech.

Instead of getting frustrated or trying to write the speech myself and having it be mediocre, I had to do more research and stay persistent in order to find the right person to accurately present my demeanor and personality. That setback taught me two things: to be comfortable with my authentic voice and how I needed to improve my interviewing skills. When I contacted other speech writers, I now knew the right questions to ask.

I found another writer who quickly understood me and the way I communicate. I delivered my speech with ease and confidence because it felt authentic. I could tell it was a hit with the crowd when people approached me afterward to share how my speech resonated with them and added their feedback.

It could happen to you

Persistence is essential if you have faced a layoff. It may surprise you, but job security is a relatively new concept in the workforce. Prior to the twentieth century, most employment was temporary. During the 1930s in the United States, labor laws provided some workers' rights and a bit more stability. By the 1960s and 1970s, companies were incentivizing employee loyalty by offering attractive benefits that included health insurance and paid time off. Workers began to feel a sense of job security, with many people spending thirty years with one company and then retiring.

As technology advances and outsourcing increases, layoffs have risen. Today, many people worry about being replaced by artificial intelligence (AI). Layoffs affect hundreds of thousands of people every year. I don't mean to draw a bleak employment picture for you; I just want to let you know that you're not that special. OK, that doesn't sound right. How about—it's not just you? You're not the only one? There is a good chance that everyone is going to get laid off sooner or later.

Although I'm joking around a bit here, hoping to make you feel better if you are one of those people who may one day get laid off, I fully recognize that, for many people, getting laid off is a traumatic experience.

Layoffs are often unexpected and frequently come at a bad time. Is there ever a good time to lose your job? It can be a devastating blow to one's ego, although layoffs have absolutely zero to do with intelligence, job performance, or company loyalty. Layoffs aren't punishments, but many people mistakenly believe they are and feel devastated by them. They question their value and their ability to find another position. *Why me? What did I do? What didn't I do? What could I have done differently? Whose feathers did I ruffle?*

You may even experience some guilt, even if you *aren't* laid off when half your team is. That dreaded feeling of waiting for the other shoe to drop quickly follows the guilt. *Am I next? When? What should I do?*

If you are laid off, give yourself time to mourn. It is not an exaggeration to say that the experience can feel a bit like a death. A key relationship in your life is suddenly gone, and you don't know how to feel or where to turn. Honor all the emotions that may arise: anger, resentment, embarrassment, fear, and, for some, a sense of relief.

There is a very disquieting sense of uncertainty when you have already witnessed one or more rounds of layoffs. Will *my job* be safe? Should I look for another job now? Some people may fear job hunting, thinking management will discover, and terminate them sooner. Once they receive notice, they can take action. With the Ninja Mindset, you will be prepared to take the next step. Your resume will be up-to-date, you will know the state of the industry, and you will have identified your strengths and your passion. Being prepared helps soften the blow.

You will need persistence to discover the benefits and resources available to you at the company and state level. You will need persistence to go through the process of finding your next position. And persistence will help you heal the emotional trauma of losing your job. Remember, persistence will help you build resilience—the ability to recover with grace and speed.

By managing your expectations around what is going to happen, you can lessen the anxiety. Some people find a job in two weeks; some people find another position in two months, and for some people, it can take up to six months or a year. Don't give up and don't compare yourself to others in the same position. Having patience will put you in the mindset to find the right job, not just the next job.

The experience of being laid off doesn't have to be completely negative. Use your ninja skills to do reconnaissance on the competition. This may be your opportunity not just to make a comfortable lateral move to another company but possibly to climb another rung on the ladder of promotion or salary. Seek out vendors or other people who worked with your organization. Think about all the different ways you can be resilient through this process.

This is the time to focus on your transferable skills. Make a list of your skills and compare them to the requirements of open positions in other companies, not just the same job title. A secondary task you perform well at one company can be a major component at a different company and be worth higher compensation. Do not equate transferable skills with parallel compensation.

Put together a schedule for when you will take specific actions for your career. Are you going to take a two-week vacation before you dive back into the job market? Are you going to apply for ten jobs every Monday? There's no wrong way to do it, but building a routine will help you focus on your goals and give you a sense of accomplishment, instead of causing you to stay up all night worrying. Find a structure that will help you maintain your persistence. Posting your résumé online will not cause a dream job to fall into your lap. What steps do you *continually* plan to take to get you where you want to be next?

Continually. You can't just do it once. Persistence is like marketing. You can't run one ad and expect results. Those ads (your efforts) have to be placed repeatedly in front of the right audience. And like marketing, you need to follow up on every lead or you will lose the sale (your next job).

What does follow-up look like on a job search? There is no place for ghosting during a job search. If you don't hear back within a week of applying, follow up with an email. You may communicate only by text in your personal life but definitely follow up an interview with an email. You want to stand out and have an edge against your competition. No one will reject you because you sent a nice thank-you note. Putting in that extra effort will show your prospective employer you are seriously interested in the job and will use the same dedication to get results if they hire you. Hiring managers may test your level of commitment and seriousness by waiting for you to reach out to them.

When you land a new job

Sometimes learning your way around a new workplace can be like learning a new language. When I landed in tech, I needed to learn the culture of the organization, which included a lot of terms that were new to me, like QBR (quarterly business review), MVP (minimum viable product), and biz dev (business development) team. I needed to be inquisitive. I had to reach out to people on several teams and introduce myself. It was the only way for me to learn about the team members and what they did at the organization. I had to join meetings and calls that I didn't necessarily need to be a part of, but I wanted to learn the broader picture. I had to identify my new company's competition and research those businesses. By asking so many questions, I became the person who had all the answers. My inquisitiveness also made me memorable to people throughout the company in a very positive way. When you ask thoughtful questions, it shows you are interested in learning and willing to invest in the quality and strength of your company and its reputation.

So what did I do with all this information? I put it together in an internal newsletter for our department, and I created an onboarding program for new hires. Then I created a document that included all the terms and acronyms along with a list of every department, its function, and how they interfaced with our team and department. I created a section that described the individual roles and how they interacted with one another. My persistence in understanding the landscape in a tech company paid off.

Word reached senior leadership that I had become an invaluable resource to help new employees get up to speed. Soon after, a facilitator from the Dublin office called to find out what I was doing.

Where did this lead? I landed a leadership role within eighteen months—because I was persistent in my search for knowledge. I was patient, waiting for the right opportunity that would place me in the spotlight.

Persistence hits the road

Like me, your dream job may include relocation, too. A new beginning. A new city. Perhaps even a new country. There are sure to be learning curves with your move. Instead of dreading them, embrace them with enthusiasm and persistence. You cannot find your way around a new neighborhood or learn a new language without intentional, applied persistence. Instead of becoming overwhelmed by your new surroundings, look at your relocation as a fun opportunity to discover new experiences and meet new people.

This will take effort on your part. Do not fall into the trap of isolating yourself because you don't know your way around: Don't fall into a cycle of work, home, food delivery, repeat.

Instead, ask questions. Your inquisitiveness will give you the opportunity to meet people and get good recommendations from the locals. Most people truly enjoy being helpful and sharing their favorite places. You can use your questions as conversation starters with coworkers, neighbors, or people you meet while out walking the dog. "Can you recommend a dry cleaner?" "Do you have a favorite Indian restaurant?" Join an online neighborhood group or a MeetUp in your new town. Crowdsourcing is your friend. Not only can you develop a list of dependable contractors and resources, but you may also wind up meeting like-minded people. I've seen online recommendations for everything from restaurants to pet sitters to jazz clubs to pickle ball courts. Making connections in a new town will help you feel connected.

New role, new team, new city

One day I swore that I would never move for a new job, yet six months later, I ended up doing just that when I moved to Chicago. New York and Chicago may both be big cities, but I quickly learned there are many differences.

I thought I was a subway pro after all my time in New York. Most of New York's system is underground. In Chicago, the subway isn't "sub" at all. A lot of it is above ground, elevated, which I quickly learned is why they call it the "L"—for elevated. In New York, the numbered streets make navigation easy. Going uptown, the numbers go up and going downtown, the numbers go down. In Chicago, there's a brown line, a pink line, and a purple line—the pink and the purple lines look an awful lot alike. The turnstiles are different in Chicago. The way you pay is different in Chicago. My first day taking the subway in Chicago had my brain spinning before I even boarded the train. *Where do I get a card? How do I refill it?* I frequently stood stock-still, looking like a deer caught in the headlights, carrying a laptop case, trying to find my way to work.

But the transportation trauma was nothing compared to the pizza. Pizza is a major topic of conversation among people from the East Coast. People sneer at you if you don't follow pizza-eating etiquette. New Yorkers like thin crust. You see, New Yorkers pick up our pizza by the wide end and fold it between our thumb and two adjacent fingers. But we don't fold it in half. We leave a channel for the steam to rise up off the cheese, which has to have a certain amount of oil (but not too much and it usually comes off the pepperoni) to make it drip just slightly off the narrow pointy end (the cheese, not the oil). You tilt your head to the side, lift the slice in front of your face, and lower to your mouth. All while carrying on a rapid conversation.

No forks and knifes! Ever! Where are we—at a banquet hall?

Chicago is famous for deep-dish pizza. Why is this even called pizza? Chicago pizza is more like a cheesy, carb-bomb quiche. I swear it's like two, three inches thick. Nevertheless, I wanted to bond with my new team of Chicagoans, so I would order pizza in for lunch on a regular basis. They would enthusiastically shovel the stuff into their mouths. Oh, the sacrifices I made. I would take a few bites, make a comment about the flavor, and pretend I liked it. Yay, team player.

Thankfully, eating less than a slice at a time of the heavy pizza didn't add a layer of blubber to my middle. Although I was happy not to gain weight, I could have used a little extra fat to keep warm—like a seal in Antarctica. Chicago may be one degree of latitude south of New York, but temperatures are much colder, so I had to buy clothes that were even warmer. My wardrobe now included clothes I hadn't known existed. I ended up with some heavily insulated pieces that were so thick it was a challenge to bend my knees and elbows.

Be persistent in making new connections, even if you are in town on a temporary basis. Social media and video calling make long-distance friendships easier to maintain than ever and they can last a lifetime. I enjoy keeping up with friends I've made all over the US and Canada.

My Case Study

Ajay is one of the many rewarding connections I've made in the course of my travels. I had the honor of coaching Ajay, and I like to call him my "Case Study." It's all right, he knows I call him that and he laughs at it.

When Ajay and I began working together, he was an account manager with an unrequited dream of advancing into sales. After a few conversations, we uncovered the root cause of his lack of success. He had a self-limiting belief: "My experience won't transfer to a new role."

We put the Five P's to work.

Ajay followed his PASSION when he worked with a mentor to help move him toward his goal. It was my role as a mentor to honor his dream and emphasize that the possibility was a realistic one.

Together, we made a PLAN to identify resources that would improve his sales skills.

Ajay had to PRIORITIZE his time to devote to additional training.

Ajay exercised PATIENCE while we found opportunities for him to partner with existing sales personnel at his company. Spending time with them, hearing about their backgrounds and experience, helped eliminate his self-limiting belief. Those conversations revealed how much he had in common with people who held the position he wanted.

He was PERSISTENT in volunteering for several stretch projects that showed the sales leaders his dedication to pursuing his passion.

He worked with his partner on the sales team and took the lead on some calls, which gave his partner the opportunity to tell the manager what a great job Ajay had done. If one of the partners was out, Ajay would close sales or upsell a product. He learned skills, practiced them, and did it without always getting credit.

Ajay had an opportunity when the next sales position opened up. He applied but didn't get the job. That's when many people would have given up, saying, "I knew I wasn't cut out for sales." Not Ajay. When the next opportunity opened up, Ajay was persistent, applied again, and that time, he got the job.

Since then, Ajay has been promoted twice.

I will leave you with these final words from Confucius. Although Confucius was a Chinese philosopher whose life predated the Japanese feudal period (12th through 19th centuries), the Japanese culture adopted his work. We can only assume that aspiring ninjas studied his work.

"It does not matter how slowly you go, so long as you do not stop."

CHAPTER 12

ASK YOURSELF IMPACTFUL QUESTIONS

In this chapter, we are going to examine the mechanics of the Five P's so you can more easily execute them and keep moving forward. That process is largely based on asking yourself questions. We all constantly look for something new, something else, something additional. It's a lot like ordering delivery when you already have enough in your refrigerator to make a satisfying meal. Sometimes it's worth calling out because you're too tired to cook. Other times, your delivery takes an hour. It's cold, missing half of what you ordered, and you deeply regret the $35 you spent on it.

You need to understand where you are before you can make a plan for where you want to go.

What do you *already* have, know, or do?

If you could use a cash infusion or want to build a financial cushion while you pursue your goals, look around you. Do you have a spare room you're not using? Rent it out. Do you have a car with an empty backseat? Become a rideshare driver. Do you have a small business and email list? You can sell your list to another company with the same type of customer base. Are you an online shopper? Add product links to your social media posts for a percentage of each sale.

What skills or opportunities are already at your fingertips? Ask yourself things like: *Whom do I know right now? What do I already know how to do?* Make use of your current degree and training before investing a great deal of time and money in more. You can use skills you already have—perhaps in a different place or way.

Find your adjacent opportunities

I had already begun working with my coach, Noreen, when I lost my job. When I told her what had happened, I was stunned and unsure of what my next step should be. She prompted me to ask myself impactful questions when she asked, "Alexis, what do you *like* to do?"

Noreen's question took me by surprise. I could easily rattle off everything on my résumé but had never thought in terms of *liking* those skills. The answer was easy: I always enjoyed traveling to other bank branches, where I trained people on how to market our programs and retain customers. Training others was just one component of my many responsibilities. That part of my job required me to learn new skills and become sufficiently competent in explaining them in a way that others could understand. It brought me fulfillment because I enjoy learning new things, connecting with other people, and helping them grow in their careers.

Noreen encouraged me to do the research and seek opportunities that would enable me to repeat the experience of educating others. I soon discovered there are companies that focus solely on training. They send people all over the world to conduct two- and three-day professional training sessions and weeklong workshops. What could be more fun than being paid to travel, meet new people, and help them gain new skills in the process?

With some research, I was able to find and land a position in the training industry with no previous industry-specific experience. I couldn't believe my new position was an actual job. It was more like a vacation. It didn't seem like work to me because it was how I dreamed of living my life—being paid to travel around the country, meet new people, spend a few days with them, and share in the learning experience. It felt like *me*—just being and breathing and making new friends. And as if this job couldn't get any better—because I worked as an independent contractor, I didn't really have a boss. Most importantly, I did not have to start at the bottom and work my way up in this new-to-me sector.

The joy I derived from coaching people in my training position at the bank motivated me to look for ways I could repeat that experience. That led me to my independent contractor training position, which increased my joy by offering more travel opportunities. As I spent more time learning the business, meeting new people, and witnessing their success, I developed passion. It was that passion that led me to take advantage of the opportunity to move to Chicago. I persevered for a year and a half to excel in my New York position before it paid off when my company offered me the management opportunity in Chicago.

That first training-focused position led me to job opportunities *adjacent* to the corporate training world, which led me to working in tech. My career has flowed successfully—from banking to corporate training to learning and development (for which I am certified) to the tech industry and also into real estate.

By asking yourself impactful questions, you can leverage your transferrable skills and adjacent opportunities when you decide to make a career change. Let's recap.

The Five P's of Success:

1. Follow your PASSION
2. Make a PLAN
3. Learn to PRIORITIZE
4. Have PATIENCE
5. Be PERSISTENT

In every one of these steps, you are going to ask yourself four questions.

- What do I need to know?
- What do I need to do?
- Whom do I need to know?
- Who do I need to be?

Remember Ajay from our previous chapter? He asked himself the four questions in each step of the process.

He asked himself, **"What do I need to know?"** He started with the requirements to be successful in a sales role.

"What do I need to do?" The answer to that question came from his research, which continued to reveal what the next action step needed to be.

"Whom do I need to know?" The answer was Alexis!—because she is going to inspire me, coach me through this process, and hold me accountable when I'm feeling frustrated or sluggish.

"Who do I need to be?" He was very clear on that—a high-earning salesperson. Someone who is willing to put in the extra work to perform tasks that weren't necessarily his responsibility, so he could learn the ropes.

What are you waiting for? There's no time like the present to get started. To get the most out of the Five P's, commit to your plan in writing. Your action outline will look like this:

The Five P's of Success:

Goal: _____

1. **Follow your PASSION**
    - What do I need to know?
    - What do I need to do?
    - Whom do I need to know?
    - Who do I need to be?

2. **Make a PLAN**
   - What do I need to know?
   - What do I need to do?
   - Whom do I need to know?
   - Who do I need to be?

3. **Learn to PRIORITIZE**
   - What do I need to know?
   - What do I need to do?
   - Whom do I need to know?
   - Who do I need to be?

4. **Have PATIENCE**
   - What do I need to know?
   - What do I need to do?
   - Whom do I need to know?
   - Who do I need to be?

5. **Be PERSISTENT**
   - What do I need to know?
   - What do I need to do?
   - Whom do I need to know?
   - Who do I need to be?

What do I need to know?

There is always more to know. From actually reading the instructions for your espresso maker before you use it to familiarizing yourself with the HOA rules before you move into a new neighborhood. A little knowledge goes a long way. A *lot* of knowledge renders exceptional results. Finding the answers to "What do I need to know?" will help you decide.

For instance, you have a passion for surfing and decide you want to move out to the West Coast so you can hit the beach every day. By researching the cost of living in Malibu, you discover this dream is out of your financial reach at the moment. Research will show you other places where the waves are gnarly and housing prices more reasonable.

What do I need to do?

Creating to-do lists will keep you on track and manage your expectations. Without a clear idea of the necessary steps to take, you may not have a realistic expectation of the time and commitment required for your task. Something as common as getting a driver's license is different in every state. It isn't difficult, but you certainly can't just show up at the DMV and hope to be issued a new license. Read the online instructions before you walk out of the house. Knowing the details—from office hours to ID requirements—will speed up your task. In some states, you don't get a laminated license the same day they issue you one. Instead, they give you a paper printout. Is that suitable ID for boarding a plane before your permanent license arrives in the mail? Ask questions to discover how your circumstances will impact you.

Whom do I need to know?

This question is frequently overlooked. You *think* you are a strong, independent person and can do it all yourself. No, you can't. We think of "Whom do you know?" as asking for help, and it is not. For instance, soaking up information is not asking for help. It's just plain smart. Being around people who have more experience or knowledge than you do is a position in which you should always place yourself. Normalize seeking assistance. One way to do this is to seek out an accountability partner or coach. Most people enjoy the opportunity to share their knowledge and like being able to offer guidance to those coming along after them. They also appreciate an outsider's or newcomer's perspective. The more people you know, the more people you can connect to each other. The more connections you make, the more help you give and receive.

Keep an open mind whenever you meet someone new. You may not immediately think you have anything in common with them, but one day that person could prove to be a useful connection or a valuable ally.

One Saturday afternoon, I found myself seated next to a pleasant and confident woman at a wedding. She introduced herself and handed me her card. Her title was "executive life coach." She talked about how much she enjoyed working with her clients and seeing them succeed.

I had never heard of a life coach at that time and did my best to keep a courteous face, thinking, *Is that even a real job?*

When I got home that night, I placed the card on my dresser. On Monday night, I picked up the card to dust the furniture (and probably throw it away) but I decided to give it another look. *Hmmm. Why not call her and find out what the job is all about?* Turns out "executive life coach" is an actual job. This is the story of how I met my coach, Noreen, who encourages me to ask myself impactful questions.

Who do I need to be?

I'm not talking about being the next Simone Biles, Brené Brown, or Michael Jordan, although I am inspired by all three. I'm talking about being the achiever of your *own* goals. I'm talking about achieving success, not fame. I'm talking about changing and enriching your own life before you set off to change the world. Be the person who listens to audiobooks in the car and at the gym. Be the person who engages with their coworkers after the meeting to ask how they successfully completed the project.

We think of our habits as our identity. We even label ourselves and then use that label as an excuse. Do you use any of these labels?

I'm not an "early riser." The time you get up in the morning is a habit, not your nature. Start your day just a half an hour earlier one or two days a week so you don't have to rush (which makes you forgetful and cranky) and have time to sit quietly while you drink your coffee or eat a healthy breakfast.

I'm not much of a "reader." There are all kinds of valid reasons people don't like to read. Some of them have to do with ADD or dyslexia. However, don't use that as an excuse to be uninformed. Find a way of gleaning information that is more suited to your learning style or lifestyle. Audiobooks, videos, webinars, and curated news services are all ways to get more information. If you don't have the time or patience to read an industry magazine, subscribe to a weekly email newsletter to stay up-to-date with the highlights. Listen to podcasts that present information in a conversational style that may be easier to remember. When you show up in a meeting and you talk about what you just read in the industry journal, you are going to impress leadership.

I'm not a "people person." You may not like large groups of people. You may not like the effort it takes to get dressed and drive across town to a networking event. But there are other ways to connect. Start by adding at least one comment to a conversation. If you are worried about sounding dumb, issue an invitation to someone who just presented by asking, "Can you expand on that?" They will appreciate the fact that you showed interest in what they had to say, and your question will give them the opportunity to talk more about a subject they are passionate about. You become likeable and memorable for giving them that opportunity.

Join one of the countless business and interest-focused groups that meet virtually. Many of them feature mastermind sessions where you can bring your questions and receive instant feedback. Some meetings have regular breakout rooms, which give you the opportunity to make valuable and targeted connections—all without leaving the house or making small talk with a stranger.

By finding alternative ways of engaging with people and contributing to a conversation, you are raising your profile. People will seek you out, which, for many of us, makes social interaction easier because we don't have to initiate the conversation.

CHAPTER 13

ARE YOU READY FOR THE NEW YOU?

If you commit to meeting your goals, it's time to give up the labels so you can become the person you *need* to be.

Do any of these statements serve you?

- I need to be the person who goes to webinars.
- I need to be the person who goes to the networking events to meet colleagues and cross-functional partners.
- I need to be the person who organizes events in the office because then I get to know everybody. (I didn't love doing this, but I got involved in the decorating committee, then moved on to major projects, and that helped me meet people from other divisions.)
- I need to be the person who asks for help.
- I need to be the person *other* people ask for help (subject-matter expert).
- I need to be the person who actually reads the industry newsletter because that is going to give me an edge.

- I need to be the person who shares my thoughts and solutions in meetings.
- I need to be the person who spends time increasing my knowledge. I will carve out one hour a week to expand my skills.

What does this new person look like?

Let's say you have decided you want to transition to being a full-time independent contractor or consultant. You began working from home during the pandemic and enjoyed the uninterrupted solitude of working from your den, which made you much more productive. It was a cost savings because you weren't filling up your gas tank every few days. You didn't have to drive in the rain for forty-five minutes and sit in a three-mile backup to get into the office. Avoiding all of those things reduced your stress level, which gave you more energy for the things you enjoy—like walking the dog and finally painting the spare bedroom. How might you use the Five P's outline to help you reach your goal?

SAMPLE WORKSHEET
Goal: Work remotely full-time
Follow your PASSION

- What do I need to know? I need to research the equipment I will need (hardware, software).
- What do I need to do? I need to make sure my family has health insurance.
- Whom do I need to know? I need to know which of my friends and family will support me through this transition.
- Who do I need to be? I need to be the person who is disciplined enough to stick to the process.

Make a PLAN

- What do I need to know? I need to identify my milestones.
- What do I need to do? Conduct a skill gap analysis.

- Whom do I need to know? I want to connect with someone who has been doing this for more than a year and will share their experience with me.

- Who do I need to be? I need to be the person who holds me accountable.

Learn to PRIORITIZE

- What do I need to know? I need to know the order I need to do these things.

- What do I need to do? I need to estimate the time needed to complete each goal.

- Whom do I need to know? I need to find an accountability partner.

- Who do I need to be? I need to be the person who makes time to complete my steps instead of watching two hours of Netflix.

Have PATIENCE

- What do I need to know? I need to know the best way to manage my expectations around my plan.

- What do I need to do? Set small, measurable goals to maintain my enthusiasm while I follow through with my plan.

- Whom do I need to know? The more research I do, the more people I meet. I need to maintain even distant relationships because those people may be able to help me in the future.

- Who do I need to be? I need to be the person who can balance enthusiasm with proper planning to make wise decisions.

Be PERSISTENT

- What do I need to know? I need to be aware of constantly changing opportunities.

- What do I need to do? I need to consider ideas outside of my vision. Researching one avenue may lead to another I never thought of. I need to refer to this list weekly to monitor my progress and remind me of my next steps.

- Whom do I need to know? I need to identify who I need to follow up with. Again.

- Who do I need to be? I need to be the person who gives me the grace and permission to fail and try again. I need to have a mindset like a child learning to walk. They fall down, fall down, fall down, and they get back up again, again, and again. When they are learning to ride a bike, they fall off, fall off, fall off, and they keep going until they learn how to ride the bike. *They* don't give up. *I* will not give up.

Be inspired

I encourage everyone to watch the Olympics. When an athlete is preparing for the Olympics, they practice, practice, practice. They got the bronze four years ago. The next year they won a silver. They don't stop there. They are going for the gold. They keep trying. When you watch the Olympic backstories, there is someone who broke their leg or tore an ACL. Instead of giving up on the Olympics, they asked, "What type of rehab do I need to get well enough to qualify for the Olympics?" You need to be the person who gives yourself enough encouragement to get back up after the inevitable stumbles. The Olympics is the strongest example of grace and permission to fail because that "failure" is a stepping stone to victory.

Now I encourage you to create your own outline and use it to write down your goal and ask the questions that will drive you toward success. The repetitiveness of the questions will force you to look at your goal from multiple perspectives, which, in turn, gives you more avenues to reach your goal. Let's take a deeper look at the questions and how they can help you stay focused.

I've used the four questions during every challenge I've faced. I asked myself "What do I need to know?" when I had to find a way out of my real estate crisis.

I asked myself "What do I need to do?" many times throughout my promotion and move to Chicago.

I constantly ask "Whom do I need to know?" in every new environment. I met colleagues and cross-functional partners in my new role.

I admit, "Who do I need to be?" had a particularly funny consequence one time. If you are like I used to be, you probably think industry journals and business magazines are strictly used to keep people distracted in waiting rooms. When I began working in finance, I decided I needed to be the person who read everything I could about business and investing. This was a good move because the knowledge I picked up while reading helped me contribute meaningful dialogue and useful suggestions in our weekly strategy sessions at the office. My managers were impressed with my insights, which made me memorable and helped propel my career forward.

One evening, a gentleman came to my home to pick me up for our first date. He sat on the couch while I walked into the kitchen to make him a drink.

When I returned to the living room, he was moving the papers and magazines around on my coffee table. He looked up at me, puzzled, and asked, "Do you really read these or did you put them out here for decoration to impress people?" Who decorates with *The Wall Street Journal* and *The Financial Times*? *Bloomberg*, *Forbes*, and *The Economist* were neatly stacked on top of the newspapers. Did he think I was trying to impress him?

I answered (a bit tartly, I admit), "Yes, I read them so I can stay well-informed about my job."

His next comment stunned me. "If these are the kinds of things you read and the conversations you have, then you're too smart for me." I could not even respond to that. Examining his insecurities is a topic for another day and a completely different book. It's no surprise that that was our last date. At least he took me to a nice place for dinner. And yes, I ordered dessert.

Hold yourself accountable

Someone once said to me, "Alexis, you don't have a *can-do* attitude; you have a *will-do* attitude." And they're right. I believe whatever it is, I'll get it done. I don't know how. I don't know where. I don't know what, but I'll get it done. I did not know how I was going to get my sister and myself out of the real estate hole, but persistence paid off. She told me just recently, "I'm not like you. I don't do well under pressure."

"I don't like it when *others* pressure me," I responded. "But I do put pressure on myself." This is inherently who I am. I also credit some of this attitude to years of working with a coach who defined the concept of "being in integrity with yourself," which I've referenced a few times in this book.

My coach, Noreen, put it this way: "There's all this integrity in dealing with other people. You keep your word here and you keep your word there. If you say you're going to do something, you do it. That's great when you promise someone else that you'll show up on time and bring cupcakes to the party. But when you are in integrity with yourself, you make goals, you follow dreams, and you take baby steps—and in the process, you keep your word to *yourself*. So just *stay true to yourself*."

If you promise yourself you are going to do something, whether it's washing the dishes before noon, putting the laundry away by the end of the day, or finishing a class you signed up for, keep your promise to yourself. By following through on the small steps and keeping your word to yourself, your dreams and goals will follow.

I frequently (*always* is probably more accurate) have several things going on at once—my day job, real estate investments, coaching, keeping my online course updated, and speaking. I'm also the landlord of four properties, which means I receive calls at all hours of the day or night about water leaks and squeaky hinges.

I also love spending a lot of time and energy being the best auntie ever by spoiling my nieces and nephews as much as possible. I'm always thinking about what I can do to bring them joy. What do they want? What do they need? What do they need but don't know they need? What will make them seem really cool to their friends? They're the center of my world.

Yet I never feel overwhelmed because I have created a plan for each goal and prioritized my tasks. Doing this keeps me from feeling pressured. I don't feel like I'm always swamped. I sleep well every night because I keep my word to myself. That means not disregarding minor tasks, minimizing my dreams, or putting off my goals.

Holding yourself accountable and asking impactful questions are ninja skills. In whatever stage of the Five P's you are in, stay focused and continue moving ahead. By doing so, you will avoid the stagnation that can come from lack of progress, laziness, or frustration. Just because your goal hasn't come into focus yet doesn't mean it is out of reach.

CHAPTER 14

WAYS FEAR CAN SHOW UP

You're not afraid of anything—except maybe losing your phone at the airport. Or losing your phone in your own home, for that matter. Because you are fearless, you are thinking about making a transition, trying something new, changing things up, or following your big dream. Maybe you've already started transitioning to a new job, a new home, a new skill, or a new relationship.

Then...

You're driving to work one morning and think, "Yeah, maybe I better put this off until I finish my degree."

You walk into the break room and see Rayna and think, "Things would be awkward between us if I got that promotion."

You are creeping along in the carpool lane and wonder if maybe you should wait to relocate until the kids are older or out of school, have graduated college, or started families of their own.

Those three scenarios of second-guessing are examples of ways fear can show up. Fear can rear its ugly head at any stage of your Five P's of Success as doubt, lack of faith, procrastination, or excuse-making. This is perfectly natural. It happens to everyone, and honestly, you might be naive if you don't experience any fear at all.

Address your fears and deal with them quickly so you can get on with the exciting changes coming your way.

When you hear the word *fear*, what comes to mind? Is it fear for your safety—like the anxiety you feel when walking to your car late at night? Does fear show up for you as nausea or stomach cramps? Do you freeze when you feel fear and are unable to move or function? Does fear show up for you as avoidance? You put off taking your car to the mechanic because you fear a big bill to replace a major component?

Let's take a quick dive into some of the ways fear may show up as you make some of life's most gratifying transitions.

Fears surrounding PASSION: Writers, influencers, and inspirational speakers everywhere tell you to "Follow your passion." What they don't share with you is that there is a very good chance you'll experience some fear surrounding your passion. After all, passion can be a powerful emotion that catches you off guard. Passion can drive your curiosity and keep you motivated when you face setbacks. But what is this thing we call *passion*? Everyone defines *passion* differently. What is passion for one person another may consider an obsession. Passion exists when you are deeply interested in an objective, devote lots of time to it, and remain motivated to pursue it despite challenges. So what is there to fear?

Become aware of your self-talk. The fearful and harsh thoughts that bubble up in your mind are a sign your ego is trying to protect you from the unknown. Whenever your internal voice badmouths you, turn that criticism into a question. Researching the answers to those questions will better prepare you for success.

For example, you may think, "I'm being selfish." Change this to "Is my passion for this goal selfish because it may take time away from my family?" In reality, your family may financially benefit from the successful business you build and the positive role model you become.

"Just because I love flowers doesn't mean I can actually make a business out of it," becomes "What type of business can I start that will allow me to work with flowers? Are there any florists in my community? Can I make a business from shipping bulbs or seeds?"

"I don't know enough to launch my own brand of bourbon." Do an online search to find out more. "Does anyone offer workshops on how to run a distillery?"

"I'm probably the only person who even likes peach salsa." This question will encourage you to collect useful data. "How do I test the market for my product?" Don't be afraid your product won't sell, verify its viability.

Fears around MAKING A PLAN: When you have any of the following thoughts, reread the chapter on planning.

"I don't know where to begin."

Don't be one of those people who never gets started. Don't be like that guy you run into at your high school reunion. He was the gearhead who spent every extra dollar on spoilers and aftermarket exhaust systems for his car. He can tell you everything about how to restore a 1967 Pontiac GTO. He helped all his friends work on their cars in exchange for a case of beer. When you chat with him over the hot buffet, you ask, "Hey, Tony, you ever open up that garage you were always talking about?"

"Oh, yeah, no. I mean, I'm looking into that. I'm talking to potential investors. Maybe one day."

Meanwhile, twenty-five years have gone by.

There is a world between MAKING A PLAN and taking action. Your first step may even be a wrong step, but it gets you on the path. Do anything. Do the wrong thing. Do the smart thing. Do the crazy thing. Just don't sit there doing nothing because you'll never get to the PRIORITIZE part of your transition if you don't start.

"I don't know how to do this."

Of course you don't. The day before Mozart ever touched a piano, he did not know how to play. Start asking questions. Seek out someone who has already succeeded in your field. If you can't meet them in person, follow them on social, read their book, listen to their podcast. How did *they* do it?

"I don't know what steps to take."

You don't have to know the entire plan. Identify just one step and take it. You will not know ahead of time everything you need to do. Don't be afraid to let the process reveal itself to you as you learn and explore.

Learn to PRIORITIZE: You are well on your way if you are experiencing fear around prioritization. This means you have shushed your ego, asked good questions, and made some kind of plan. Now you have a lot of things on your plate and need to figure out the order in which to do them.

When in doubt as to how to organize your schedule, default to Maslow's Hierarchy of Needs, which drives human behavior:

1. Physiology
2. Safety
3. Love and Belonging
4. Esteem
5. Self-actualization

Physiology. Remember to eat and get enough rest. I am not kidding about this. Don't fall victim to the "grind culture"—skipping meals and working yourself to exhaustion. This is mentally counterproductive because it negatively impacts your health. Without proper nutrition, you get sick more easily. Without sufficient rest, your brain does not work as well.

Safety. Avoid risks that jeopardize the place you live. (Make sure you set aside enough money to pay the rent or mortgage.) This means creating a budget and sometimes staying in your day job until you have built a financial cushion.

Love and Belonging. Take care of your loved ones. This includes everything, from attending Little League games to honoring date night with your partner to calling your mother every Sunday. The people you love are a vital support system and they need you, too. You may get busy, but make time for the people who were with you before you set foot on the path of your big dream and will be there to celebrate your success.

Esteem. Staying committed (persistence) to your plans and goals builds your self-esteem when you see what you are capable of and can accomplish. You will be learning constantly and your knowledge and skill will earn you respect from others.

Self-actualization. This is the deep satisfaction of realizing your dreams.

After you honor your basic needs, you can create schedules for all the other things you need to do. Start with hard deadlines, like license applications and appointments. If you are building a house, the building inspector has to approve the wiring and plumbing before you can put up the walls. This means that even if your drywall installer is available this week, you may have to wait until their next window of opportunity the following month. A two-week delay now may save you money and time if you have to replace faulty wiring. It makes no sense to rip out drywall to get your rough-ins up to code.

Begin with necessary tasks and follow with the fun stuff. It might be fun to go shopping for furniture for your new house, but it is wiser to wait until you have a firm completion date so you have a place to put it. In other words, don't put the cart before the horse—or the recliner before the roof.

If you are creating a side gig and you see a lot of potential for it one day replacing your full-time job, that's an exciting thing. Don't get swept away in that potential, though. Your current employer is still paying your bills and providing your security. Don't jeopardize that by allowing your passion project to derail you at work. You need to show up every day and deliver your best work. I have read many stories of people turning former employers into future clients—another reason to maintain good relationships with your employers and coworkers.

There will be many times when your employer, your family, your health, your commitments—must take priority over your project. Don't be afraid to *rearrange* your priorities.

Have PATIENCE. Fears around patience can often show up in the form of FOMO, the fear of missed opportunities. This is a time when The Career Ninja Mindset® will serve you well.

If, for example, you want to change jobs, it can be an exciting and stressful experience. If you are unhappy at your current position or you do not have job security, it can be very tempting to accept the first offer. You just want to get out of there. Perhaps you feel undervalued: The highest-salary offer can woo you into making the wrong move. You may have recruiters filling your inbox with lots of opportunities that make you feel in demand, but don't match your goals. It is important to keep sight of your goal, which should never be "just getting another job."

Ask yourself why you want to change jobs and what you want to achieve, then measure every opportunity against that. This is where patience is essential. The first offer you receive may be in your comfort zone, with a salary similar to what you currently earn. But does it provide an opportunity to learn or advance?

When making decisions about your next job, remember to explore adjacent opportunities. For instance, a sales position in one company may have a greater potential than a marketing position in another company. You may encounter a sales opportunity that has a low base pay or draw against commission. A mid-level marketing position at the same company starts at a higher salary, but caps lower than a commission potential. For someone who wants a predictable income, the marketing job may be the best choice. For someone who thrives on effort equaling compensation, the sales job will offer them greater personal reward with potentially higher income.

In another company, moving from sales to marketing could offer additional training, benefits, travel opportunities, and more rapid growth potential, even though the initial salary is lower.

Fear or excitement can tempt you into decisions that do not meet your goal or serve your long-term objectives. It requires patience to wait for multiple offers and thoroughly research them. Don't be afraid of missing the *wrong* opportunity.

Be PERSISTENT. Fear around persistence can sound like, "Am I nagging that person? Is this plan hopeless? I'm not seeing any progress. Should I change my goal? Does anybody care? Maybe I should just give up."

There will be days when you are tired. You are tired of delays and rejection. You are tired of dead ends. You are frustrated by slow progress. You come home, flop on the couch, look the dog in the eye, and say, "I should just give up." If you're lucky, your dog will put his paw on your shoulder, lick your face, and remind you, you are doing all this for him. Your passion is to start your own business, so you never have to leave him home alone again. Cats are a lot less supportive of your dreams, but still grateful for the effort you put into the work.

Without dogged persistence (See what I did there?), there would be no Harry Potter books. J.K. Rowling was turned down by twelve publishers before finding one who would take her on. Stephen King was turned down by nearly thirty publishers. The movie *Avatar: The Way of Water* was in production for twelve years before it hit the screen. And none of those stories compare to that of Jack Canfield, author of The Chicken Soup series. Chances are you have read one of his books—the Chicken Soup for the Soul series has over 275 titles, including: *Chicken Soup for the College Soul, Chicken Soup for the Entrepreneur's Soul,* and *Chicken Soup for the Grieving Soul.* Jack was turned down by 123 publishers. Jack Canfield is the soul of persistence.

Don't be afraid of rejection.

Now here's one, you may not see coming but might totally identify with it: **Fear of Success**. Sounds crazy, right? Who would be afraid of achievement and abundance and recognition? Trust me, it's real because I have had these thoughts. And this is the kind of self-talk that showed up for me.

If I am successful, is it going to change my life dramatically in negative ways? Am I going to be traveling more? If I become a successful speaker, I'm going to be on the road with a lot of people and attending big conventions. After my last bout with COVID, I have a fear of doing too much and getting exhausted.

What if I push myself too far with all the international flying I do? It takes three, four, or five days for my body to recover from a trip to the West Coast. I have to be crammed in a plane with five hundred sneezing, coughing people for five hours. Will success negatively impact my health?

I worry that the success of being a speaker and coach will be draining, and I won't have time to spoil all of my nieces and nephews the way they're used to me doing.

You may worry that your success will take time away from your kids or somehow negatively impact your marriage. Do you think success will change you—and not for the better? Will you get what my grandmother calls "too big for your britches"?

Now that I'm middle-aged, I have asked myself, *Can I really do this?* I'm pretty sure I can handle it, but the fear does creep in.

Martha Stewart started her company at age fifty. At age sixty-four, she was sent to federal prison for fraud. She rebounded her business within a year of her release. At age eighty-one, she appeared on the cover of the *Sports Illustrated Swimsuit Issue*. She is definitely a woman fueled by Passion. Martha is the Queen of Making a Plan, knows how to Prioritize, has the Patience to weather the storms, and has Persisted her way to an estimated worth of $400 million. So I guess I don't need to worry about age—and neither should you.

OK, I put this one off until last. Fear can surface as procrastination. If you have made your transition decision and aren't taking any steps toward your goal, that is procrastination. There will most likely never be a time in your life when you have no other commitments and nothing but free time. However, we all know people who are doing twelve things at once and doing them successfully. They don't procrastinate.

Recognizing and overcoming fear is another Ninja Mindset skill you can develop. If you come up against any fear, or feel like your progress is stagnating, go back and look at your Five P's worksheet. Reread your goals and create new ones as necessary. Remember, you are learning something new with every step of your journey, so it is only natural that strategies will shift and new hurdles will need to be overcome.

CHAPTER 15

LIMITING BELIEFS

O ver the last ten years of working with my business coach, I have expressed a lot of the fears that have arisen along with my success. Recently, we discussed something you hear a lot about on social media: imposter syndrome. The term is used to describe the doubt experienced by high-achieving people. These individuals are afraid other people will think they are unqualified frauds. To me, imposter syndrome is nothing more than a fear of success combined with poorly managed expectations.

Women, especially, experience imposter syndrome when they take on a new role because they think that they're supposed to know everything. But they're not. When you get to a new job or you get promoted or you join a team, you're not an imposter; you are new. You are not supposed to know everything.

You're new to the role when you get married. You're new to being a spouse. It's the first time you've done it. So you're not being an imposter; you are figuring it out. You will learn and adapt to any change in your life. You will need to learn and adapt if you change companies, even though you're still in the same industry that you've spent the last twenty years in. If you change industries, you are not going to be comfortable, so it is important to remind yourself you are not supposed to know everything. If you feel like you don't belong in the room or at the table, it's because others have treated you like you don't belong there. That can psychologically impact you, but that doesn't make it a fact.

Imposter syndrome is a limiting belief

There is a common thread in all the examples I've mentioned. Every one of them involves change. Nearly three-quarters of the population experience fear of change in varying degrees, from discomfort to complete avoidance at all costs. Do you know someone who has gone to the same place every year for vacation—for twenty years? Are you one of those people who won't upgrade your phone because you just know it won't work right, meaning it will function differently than the old model. Does the thought of downloading a new app make you groan? Do you fear changing your dentist, hairstylist, or accountant, even though you're dissatisfied with their service?

I am guilty of this somewhat. I'm not *afraid* of change—let's just say it disgruntles me. I recently got a new car. You would think having the latest model would excite me, but no. I dragged my feet until the last possible moment. The lease was up on my old car, and I wound up getting the exact same model, just the newer version, because I didn't want to have to learn a new car. I drive an SUV, and I don't really need all that space, but I did not opt for a smaller, sportier model because I did not want to learn all the new bells and whistles on an unfamiliar vehicle.

And can we talk about the grocery store for a minute? You run in to pick up your usual items. You've brought a to-go cup of coffee and congratulate yourself on actually remembering your shopping list this time. You grab your cart, turn right, and nearly run into a cardboard display of air fresheners. What is that doing in the middle of the aisle? Everything has moved. There are bagels where the pickles should be. Nothing is where you normally find it. You feel justified at your angry outburst as the produce clerk scurries away from you.

How many people's careers are stalled because they fear change? My sister's friend has been in the insurance business for over twenty years.

I see her a few times a year at parties or girls' night out and we basically have the same conversation every time.

> Me: How's the job?
>
> Sandra: Could be better. I got passed over for a promotion—again.
>
> Me: Why don't you find another job?
>
> Sandra: You know how tough the job market is.
>
> Me: Have you updated your résumé?
>
> Sandra: Things have changed so much. I wouldn't know what to put on mine any more.
>
> Me: You can hire someone to do that for you.
>
> Sandra: That's too expensive.
>
> Me. Try Fiverr.

That was four years ago. Sandra actually updated her résumé (herself) and applied to a few jobs online. A buyout of her company brought in new managers, who then also denied her a promotion.

> Sandra: I'm just lucky I still have a job.
>
> Me: What do you mean?
>
> Sandra: It's my accent. That's what's holding me back really.
>
> Me: What are you talking about? You live in New York. Everybody has an accent.
>
> Sandra: You think? Well, they posted an opening for a job I would really like. It would be a promotion and a transfer to another division. I could even work from home about half the time.
>
> Me: That's great! You should definitely go for it.

I really like Sandra. She's smart and capable (and kills at karaoke) but I get frustrated with her. I know she has transferrable skills, and it would be so good for her self-esteem to get this promotion. I'm getting excited for her.

But she keeps talking.

> Sandra: I dunno. What would the underwriters think? It would be kind of awkward with Judy if I got the job.

That's it. I give up. Not only does she fear change. She is apparently also afraid of what other people will think.

I'm going to tell you a little story about how *I* feel about what *other people* think.

The downtown high-rise where my office is located has a security guard posted at the front door. The main security guard is one of those alarmingly friendly guys. Most days he is busily chatting up other people. Last week, I arrived a little bit earlier than usual and the lobby was relatively empty. Twenty or thirty snowflakes had fallen, and I guess a lot of people were working from home, but I bundled up and headed into the office. He spotted me and started walking with me toward the bank of elevators. At this point, he offered me this advice: "Good morning. Hey, I hope you don't take this the wrong way. I don't mean to insult you, but you look much better when you dress up for work. You know, professional."

I smiled and let him finish. "Oh, you haven't insulted me at all." He must have thought, *Aha, this woman must really be impressed with my fashion sense.*

I continued, "You can't insult me because I don't value your opinion on my clothes, and I didn't ask for it."

He has offered no fashion advice since.

How much value do *you* place on other people's opinions about your life, business, choices, health, family, or relationships? Do you make decisions based on what someone else thinks?

It is easy to be swayed by the opinions of those we love or respect—even those who have no experience with the topic they are speaking about. You may want to please them or fear their reaction if you don't follow their direction. How often have you made a decision that wasn't in your best interest just to "keep the peace"?

It is a skill to discern the difference between wisdom that will benefit you and opinion based on someone else's experience and biases.

There are some questions you can ponder before you follow someone else's advice or acquiesce to their position:

- Are they sharing a previous experience you can learn from or are they repeating dogma?
- Do they have your best interest in mind or are they trying to impress you with their knowledge?
- Are they trying to exert power over you?
- Did you seek out their advice or did they offer it unsolicited—like the security guard?

How long will the impact last? Is it the opinion of a coworker you will only see rarely after you get the promotion or maybe never again? Is it the reaction of a parent who is unhappy with your choice, sighs into the phone, and rolls their eyes at you during the family dinner—but then is the first one to brag about your success to all of their friends?

Other people's opinions are often based on their own fears. They would never dream of moving across the country and project all of their fear onto your dream. They will emphasize how much trouble it is and how much you will miss your regular coffee shop and how difficult it is to make new friends. It is possible they are jealous of your confidence or opportunities that have come your way.

Do not let your fear of what other people think stand in the way of your dreams. Give their opinions the proper weight. They could have real-life experience to share or raise issues that you'd be wise to consider.

Factual information is different from useful information. If someone tells you, "Three out of five new restaurants fail in the first year," it may be factual information, but does it help you? Whereas giving you a link to a list of Small Business Administration loans and grants is useful information from a supportive friend.

And if you are doing business on social media, most of your followers and commentators are not your friends. You will probably never meet most of them. Do not live your life for strangers. Are they going to pay your bills? Are they going to hug you? Are they going to loan you money? Are they pursuing their own dream or just trolling yours? The online space is not real. Don't let trends and strangers dictate your self-esteem.

There is an intersection between imposter syndrome (which is just a limiting belief) and fear of other people's opinions. Many people experience overwhelming doubts when they have just gotten a promotion or landed a new account. They have met their goal and suddenly lose faith in their abilities or performance. If you catch yourself feeling this way, remind yourself of what you have already gone through and learned to get to where you are right now.

If you've made it through three rounds of interviews internally or externally and they've hired you, you deserve the role. Don't let Karen's opinion of whether you'll be a good manager enter your mind. You deserve the role. Karen's thoughts about whether you deserve the role are irrelevant because the decision-makers at the organization have already chosen you. Negative people will always want to rain on your parade. They are the people who stay stuck in their roles and never achieve anything because everyone around them perceives their negativity, and it holds them back. Don't fear the Karens!

CHAPTER 16

FILL YOUR CUP

This book has given you a lot to think about, and I hope a lot of inspiration, motivation, guidance, and at least twenty new things to add to your to-do list. And now I want to circle back to where we started—joy. Throughout all your hard work, planning, and persistence, never lose sight of your joy. Find ways to feel joy every day. Every day.

From the time you started reading this book until we are here, at the end—have you discovered, reignited, or even changed your sources of joy?

The key is to find joy where you are. We live in a society that has normalized dissatisfaction. No one expects you to like your job or even your life. And believe me, marketers are banking on your dissatisfaction. They want you to be unhappy with what you drive, where you live, the clothes you wear, and especially the way you look. It takes a very healthy sense of self to be able to shake off the constant pressure of manufactured dissatisfaction. There are two immediate and easy steps you can take that will reduce dissatisfaction and increase joy: Stop comparing yourself to others, and be grateful for what you already have. You are perfect just the way you are.

Now that you have adopted The Career Ninja Mindset® you have the tools to overcome any challenge and can leverage any true dissatisfaction into motivation to pursue your dream.

Finding satisfaction, whether it is in your career or your personal life, is entirely up to you. Despite what the commercials would have you believe, a new watch or the latest drug won't magically and instantly make everything OK.

Finding joy is as important to your self-care as proper nutrition and rest. One of the ways I find joy is by what I call "filling my cup." It is especially important to fill your cup while you manifest your next great opportunity.

Keep a growth mindset

If you don't believe you can learn something new, you won't. A growth mindset doesn't just refer to learning a new skill. It means keeping your mind open to new ideas and different beliefs. Truly listening to other people. I did not get to where I am today by going it alone. And you shouldn't either. Apply The Career Ninja Mindset® to every goal you want to accomplish.

One way to expand your mind and reach your goals faster is to work with a coach or mentor. I have worked with many over the years. Some I've consulted briefly for a specific goal and I've worked with Noreen for many years. She encourages me, holds me accountable, and sometimes believes in me when I've lost a little faith in myself. In addition to working with her, I also have a coach to help me with my speaking business, because that is where I want to focus my energy going forward and Suzanne is an expert in that arena.

Too often we're told that breakthroughs come when we step back and sit with ourselves, but experience has taught me that that's not the best, most efficient, or most effective way to deal with challenges and growth.

A good coach or mentor will not tell you what to do. They're going to help you recognize the passion and potential within you that you might not even know is there. A good coach is someone who can see your potential, even when you doubt yourself. They are also a partner who will help you stay accountable. It's easy to make plans and set goals—it's a lot harder to follow through on them day after day, week after week. A coach or mentor is there to keep you on track.

The success and growth I've seen in myself encouraged me to become a coach, too. I truly want to help others pursue their passions, avoid some of the pitfalls, and celebrate their success with them.

Continue to seek knowledge

You don't always need to earn another degree. You may just need to get a certification in your field. Learning isn't just for career advancement. The internet literally gives you access to a world of knowledge. I'm convinced you can learn how to do just about anything on YouTube. Need to change a faucet? There's a video for that. Want to move to another country? There's a Facebook group that will list all the documents you need and a timeline for completion. Want to lead seminars around the world? There's a free online webinar that will teach you how. Online learning and community colleges are excellent educational resources. In contrast to traditional academic settings, instructors at online universities and community colleges, in many cases, are still actively employed in the field, have the most useful advice, and are versed in the latest tools and policies. No time spent on learning is ever wasted.

Help someone else succeed

Become a mentor. You don't need to join a program or nonprofit to do this. You can take the new person at your office under your wing. You will come to realize you know more than you thought and get satisfaction from watching another person grow. What you put out into the universe comes back to you. As I gained recognition for creating the onboarding program and newsletter for my division, you, too, can expect recognition for your selflessness.

Spend time with your family and friends

Stay engaged with the people you love. They are your constant. They will hold you accountable and cheer you on. They provide a distraction from your hard work. Although I love advancing through my career, spending time with my family and friends is where I find my true joy. It is nice to put the spreadsheets aside for a while and leave space to laugh and cry, look at family photos, eat my mother's home cooking, and have a good chat with my sister and brother. I set aside special time to spend with my nieces and nephews. They really keep me grounded.

Volunteer

Volunteering broadens and enriches your life in so many more ways than I can list here. You make new friends, learn new skills, help a worthy cause, and lift others up. Volunteering is a perfect way to put all your learning to work to benefit others. Make sure you add your volunteer activities to your résumé or CV. They highlight additional skillsets and reflect you are a well-rounded, compassionate individual.

Be alone with your own thoughts

Quiet time is important. I don't mean you have to join a Zen monastery and spend hours in uncomfortable, silent meditation. Some people find it difficult to be alone. They need the constant stimulation of other people and their ideas. But unless you devote some time to solitude, you will not be able to discern your own thoughts and beliefs from those of the people around you—who are more than happy to tell you what *they* think you should do and believe. Being alone leaves the door open to recognize your own desires and beliefs.

Get enough rest

If you are staying up late working, you are doing yourself an injustice. Pushing through when you are tired causes mistakes. You do not do your best thinking when you are tired. When you are wiped out, stop. If you are being honest with yourself, you will recognize when your brain has hit its limit for the day. Instead of grinding away with sub-par work and poor ideas, put your project aside and get some sleep. When you wake refreshed, the ideas will flow faster and easier. You also need sufficient sleep to maintain your immune system and regulate your emotions. Lack of sleep is bad for your heart, can lower your sex drive, and lead to anxiety and depression. Look at those symptoms I just mentioned. Some people pop a pill for every one of them when getting enough sleep might prevent them in the first place—so get some rest.

Take care of your health

Listen to your body; it is smarter than you are. Don't ignore symptoms or persistent discomfort. Your body is trying to warn you to pay attention now or pay the price later with more serious consequences. When you are sick, stay home and give yourself time to heal. You need rest and hydration to recover. A wonderful gift you can give to others is to stay away from them when you are sick.

Celebrate your victories—especially the small ones

Did you hit a deadline? Celebrate! Did you make the meeting on time? Congratulate yourself. Did you remember to put the kids' uniforms in their backpacks? Yay you. If you think you should only celebrate the big goals, like getting a new job, graduating college, or earning a generous salary, you set yourself up for disappointment. In many cases, by the time you finally hit that goal, you feel almost let down—like, now what? You set yourself up for the need for massive, hard-to-reach goals and live life in dissatisfaction during the years in between. Celebrating the little wins raises your vibe and keeps you going. It also improves your self-esteem.

Do something creative and fun

Activities like painting and cooking engage the right side of the brain, and stimulating the right side of the brain improves problem-solving skills. Participating in activities that use both sides of the brain, like solving jigsaw puzzles, helps with cognitive function and increases your attention span. Never underestimate the curative properties of fun, laughter, letting go, being silly, dancing, and singing. Join a team. Stay active. Play a sport. Get those endorphins (the body's natural feel-good chemicals/hormones) flowing. Having fun reduces stress, improves your mood, and helps you sleep. A happy, healthy you will reach your goals faster than an exhausted shell of a human. Maintaining a good sense of humor keeps your stress levels down and lightens the mood for the people around you.

Remember, The Career Ninja Mindset® isn't about having all the answers. It's about asking the right questions and being willing to put in the work to find the answers. The world isn't slowing down—the question is, are you going to keep up or get left behind?

Begin your journey by excelling where you are. By doing that, you will polish your reputation, come to appreciate what you already have, and build skills that will help you with whatever transition you choose next.

This book isn't about how to get promoted, but if you follow the Five P's, you could get promoted. This book isn't about changing jobs, but if you follow the process, this book will help you change jobs. This book isn't specifically about starting a new business. This book is about outlining the steps you can take to move toward achieving your dreams and goals.

Hopefully, some of the stories I've shared here have inspired you. Maybe it was the way my grandmother moved to this country with two children and saved enough money to buy her own home within five years. Or the way I found a path to dig my sister and myself out of a financial hole. Perhaps you admired the way my friend Malik walked away from the law profession to pursue his passion for cooking.

I'm going to end this book with a challenge—and that's for each of you to adopt The Career Ninja Mindset®.

Commit to three concrete actions you will take in the next month to move your big goal forward. Maybe it's reaching out to someone you admire for a coffee chat. Maybe it's signing up for an online course to learn a new skill. Maybe it's volunteering to lead a project at work that's outside of your comfort zone. Whatever it is, commit to it. Put it in your calendar.

Tell a friend or colleague about it so they can hold you accountable. Knowing what you need to do is only half the battle. The other half is actually doing it. Even if it's a small thing, you must execute it to make progress. Every action, no matter how big or small, moves you forward.

Here's something to think about as you read this last page. Suppose I write a second edition of this book and include *your* story. What would it be? How did you use The Career Ninja Mindset® skills to follow your dream and achieve your goals?

Wishing you the best of luck,
Alexis
[contact info www.alexiskingconsulting.com]

www.ingramcontent.com/pod-product-compliance
Lightning Source LLC
Chambersburg PA
CBHW060932220326
41597CB00020BA/3724